Nice
Spells

Simple & Sweet

Skye Alexander

Adams Media
Avon, Massachusetts

Published by Adams Media, an F+W Publications Company
57 Littlefield Street
Avon, MA 02322
www.adamsmedia.com

ISBN: 1-59337-631-6
Printed in Canada.

J I H G F E D C B A

Library of Congress Cataloging-in-Publication Data

Alexander, Skye.
Naughty spells/nice spells / Skye Alexander.
p.   cm.
ISBN 1-59337-631-6
1. Magic. 2. Charms. I. Title.
BF1611.A445 2006
133.4'4--dc22
                                                    2006013594

This publication is designed to provide accurate and authoritative information with regard to the subject matter covered. It is sold with the understanding that the publisher is not engaged in rendering legal, accounting, or other professional advice. If legal advice or other expert assistance is required, the services of a competent professional person should be sought.

> —From a *Declaration of Principles* jointly adopted by a
> Committee of the American Bar Association and
> a Committee of Publishers and Associations

Many of the designations used by manufacturers and sellers to distinguish their product are claimed as trademarks. Where those designations appear in this book and Adams Media was aware of a trademark claim, the designations have been printed with initial capital letters.

Interior Art © Dover Publications.

This book is available at quantity discounts for bulk purchases.
For information, please call 1-800-872-5627.

To R.L., who shared his magick I with me

contents

Miscellaneous Spells **63**

Introduction

What Is Magick?

The Buddha taught that we create the world with our thoughts. In a sense, he was describing the magickal process, for the mind is the most important factor in magickal work. Here's another way to look at it. Before something can materialize in the physical world, somebody must first imagine it. An architect envisions a house before it can be built. You do the same thing when you perform magick—you create a mental image of the result you intend to produce, then fuel it with your willpower and emotion. You are the architect of your own life.

Of course, to build a house you need hammers, saws, and other tools. In magick, spells are the "tools" you use to fabricate your wishes. When you do a spell, you activate your own creative energy and blend it with the energies embodied by the ingredients that you use in the spell—plants, gemstones, etc.—in order to shape an outcome. Energy, as you know, is the raw material that makes up our Universe. By molding energy through the use of spells, rituals, and other magickal practices, you literally create your own reality.

As you perform the spells in this book, remember that magick isn't inherently dangerous, or evil, or difficult. In fact, you're doing magick all the time, whether or not you realize it. The important thing is to be aware of your thoughts, emotions, and actions, and to use your magickal power with clear intent, so you can produce the results you truly desire.

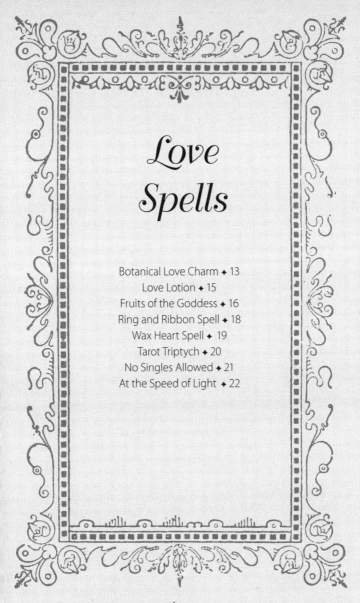

Love Spells

Botanical Love Charm

rating: **silver**

This simple charm taps the energies of the plant kingdom to help you attract the right person into your life.

Best times to perform this spell:

+ During the waxing moon
+ When either the sun or moon is in Libra
+ On Fridays

Ingredients or equipment needed:

+ A circle of red silk cloth, 6 inches in diameter
+ A pink ribbon 6 inches long
+ 2 red rose petals
+ 2 raspberry leaves
+ 2 myrtle flowers
+ 2 apple seeds
+ A piece of paper
+ A pen with red ink

1. On the piece of paper, write:

> *"This charm brings me a lover who is right
> for me in every way."*

2. Fold the paper three times, then place it and botanicals in the center of the silk circle.

3. Tie up the cloth to make a pouch containing the ingredients.

continued

4. Tie six knots in the ribbon, and repeat your intention aloud each time you tie a knot.

5. Carry the love charm in your pocket or purse during the day and put it under your pillow at night, until your wish comes true.

Love Lotion

rating: **silver**

Use this sweet-smelling lotion to sweeten
a relationship with your beloved.

Best times to perform this spell:
- During the waxing moon
- When either the sun or moon is in Taurus or Libra
- On Fridays

Ingredients or equipment needed:
- 2 ounces of grape seed, olive, or almond oil
- 2 dried red or pink rose petals, crushed very finely
- 1/8 teaspoon of melted honey
- 1/2 teaspoon apple cider
- 2 drops of jasmine, rose, ylang-ylang, or patchouli essential oil
- A pink, purple, or red glass bottle or jar

1. Blend all ingredients together and pour the mixture into the glass bottle or jar. (If you can't find a pink, purple, or red container, clear glass will suffice.)

2. Set the bottle on a windowsill where the moon can shine on it and leave it there overnight.

3. Put a drop of Love Lotion on your heart and wrists each morning—you'll send out loving vibrations with each heart-beat.

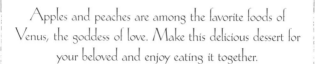

Fruits of the Goddess

rating: **silver**

Apples and peaches are among the favorite foods of
Venus, the goddess of love. Make this delicious dessert for
your beloved and enjoy eating it together.

Best times to perform this spell:
+ Anytime

Ingredients or equipment needed:
+ A 9-inch piecrust
+ 3–4 apples
+ 3–4 cups fresh peaches
+ 1/3 cup brown sugar
+ 1/3 cup granulated sugar
+ 2 rounded tablespoons flour
+ 1/2 teaspoon cinnamon
+ 1/4 teaspoon nutmeg
+ 1/8 teaspoon salt
+ 2 tablespoons butter or margarine
+ 9-inch pie pan
+ A paring knife

1. Preheat oven to 425 degrees. Combine all dry ingredients in a small bowl.

2. Peel the apples and peaches, remove cores and pits, and slice the fruit.

3. Arrange half of the fruit slices in the piecrust, then sprinkle half the sugar mixture over the fruit. Dot with half the butter.

4. Repeat, using the rest of the fruit, sugar mix, and butter.

5. Bake about 45 minutes, or until the fruit and crust are lightly browned. (Cover with foil for part of the time if the crust seems to be browning too fast.)

Ring and Ribbon Spell

rating: **fog**

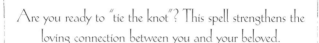

Are you ready to "tie the knot"? This spell strengthens the loving connection between you and your beloved.

Best times to perform this spell:
+ During the waxing moon
+ When the sun or moon is in Libra
+ On Fridays

Ingredients or equipment needed:
+ 2 rings
+ A piece of red or pink ribbon
+ A pen that writes on fabric

1. Write your name and your partner's on the ribbon, along with a special loving wish.

2. Slip the ribbon through the two rings and tie a knot, while you envision your wish coming true.

3. Tie the ribbon and rings on your bedroom doorknob.

Wax Heart Spell

rating: **silver**

This spell is sure to melt your beloved's heart.

Best times to perform this spell:

+ During the waxing moon
+ When the sun or moon is in Libra
+ On Fridays

Ingredients or equipment needed:

+ 2 red or pink candles
+ Matches
+ A ballpoint pen
+ Aluminum foil
+ Love Lotion (see page 15)

1. With the pen, carve your name in one candle and your beloved's in the other.

2. Light both candles, then tilt them so the melting wax drips onto the foil, blending to form a single mound of wax.

3. Add a few drops of the Love Lotion. When you have enough wax to mold, allow it to cool slightly, but don't let it harden.

4. Form a heart out of the wax. Place the wax heart on your bedside table. If you prefer, you can insert a wick into the wax heart and use it as a candle to fire up your romance.

Tarot Triptych

rating: **fog**

A triptych is an altarpiece or decoration composed of three panels, in this case, tarot cards, joined together.
Let the vibrant imagery of the tarot bring you the love and happiness you desire.

Best times to perform this spell:

+ During the waxing moon
+ When the sun or moon is in Libra
+ On Fridays

Ingredients or equipment needed:

+ 3 tarot cards
+ Scotch tape
+ Essential oil of rose, jasmine, patchouli, ylang-ylang, or musk

1. To make a love triptych, choose three cards from a tarot deck (one you don't use for readings). These cards should depict things you desire in a romantic relationship (see Appendix F for more information). For instance, you might choose the 10 of Pentacles if financial security is important to you or the Ace of Cups if you want to attract a new partner.

2. Lay the cards face down, side-by-side, and tape them together. Then stand the triptych up in a place where you'll see it often. (If you know feng shui, put it in the Relationship Gua.)

3. Dab some essential oil on each card, while you envision yourself enjoying the loving relationship you seek.

No Singles Allowed

rating: **silver**

The symbolism in this ritual is obvious!

Best times to perform this spell:
✦ During the waning moon

1. Go through your drawers, closets, etc. and get rid of solo items that once were part of a pair—toss those lone socks, gloves, earrings, and anything else that has lost its mate. Put these items into a trash bag, and tie it up with a black ribbon. Bury it on the night before the new moon. This symbolic act demonstrates your intention to end your single status and welcome a romantic partner into your life.

At the Speed of Light
rating: **fog**

Here's a quick and easy way to communicate with a loved one, even if you can't reach him/her via the usual methods.

Best times to perform this spell:
+ Anytime

1. Calm and center yourself. Close your eyes and bring your beloved's image to mind. Visualize this person sitting in front of you. Imagine a beam of light flowing from your solar plexus to your lover's solar plexus, connecting the two of you. This ray of light is a conduit through which you can communicate instantaneously, using the language of pictures.

2. In your mind's eye, create an image that expresses what you wish to say to your lover, then send it through the conduit of light. Feel the light beam vibrating as your message is conveyed to the other person.

3. Now, empty your mind and allow yourself to receive a reply—that reply may come in the form of pictures, feelings, sensations, or words.

4. When you've finished your "conversation," say goodbye, retract the ray of light into yourself, and open your eyes.

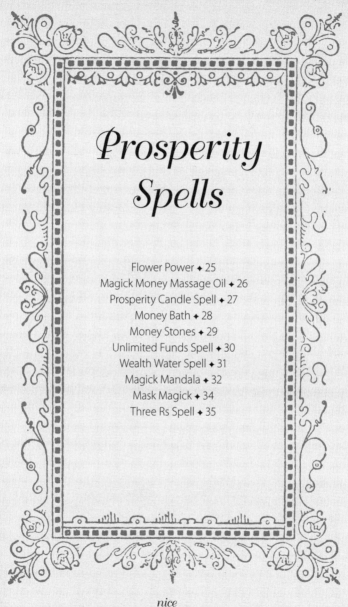

Prosperity Spells

Flower Power

rating: **silver**

Increase your chances for prosperity with this spell that uses symbolic imagery to make your wealth "grow."

Best times to perform this spell:

+ During the waxing moon
+ When the sun or moon is in Taurus
+ On Thursdays

Ingredients or equipment needed:

+ Marigold plants
+ Silver coins (any denomination)

1. The marigold's circular yellow blooms remind us of golden coins. Plant marigold seedlings in your yard, in window boxes, or flowerpots.

2. Put a silver coin beneath each plant. Focus on your objective—to attract prosperity—while you work. As the flowers blossom, so will your fortune.

Magick Money Massage Oil

rating: **silver**

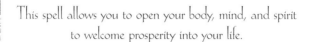

This spell allows you to open your body, mind, and spirit
to welcome prosperity into your life.

Best times to perform this spell:
+ During the waxing moon
+ When the sun or moon is in Taurus
+ On Thursdays

Ingredients or equipment needed:
+ 8 ounces of grape seed, olive, or almond oil
+ 3 drops of essential oil of cedar
+ A pinch of dried peppermint
+ 3 whole cloves
+ A silver coin
+ A small piece of aventurine
+ A green glass jar or bottle

1. Pour the vegetable oil into the jar or bottle.

2. Add the peppermint, essential oil, and cloves.

3. Add the coin and the aventurine. Put a top on the jar or
bottle and shake it three times while you envision money
coming your way.

4. Every morning, massage your palms and the soles of
your feet with the oil. Pay special attention to the Mounds of
Venus, where your thumbs join your palms.

5. Put a drop of oil on each of the areas associated with your
seven major chakras to attract riches of all kinds.

Prosperity Candle Spell

rating: **silver**

This spell lights the way to prosperity and brightens your financial prospects.

Best times to perform this spell:

+ Begin eight days before the full moon
+ Begin when the sun or moon is in Taurus

Ingredients or equipment needed:

+ A green or gold candle
+ Candleholder
+ Ballpoint pen
+ A few drops of Magick Money Massage Oil (see page 26)
+ Matches

1. With the pen, carve words such as "abundance," "money," "wealth," and "riches" on the candle, along with your own name.

2. Pour a little Magick Money Massage Oil in your palm and rub it on the candle, coating everything except the wick.

3. Put the candle in a candleholder and set it in a safe place. Light the candle, gaze into the flame, and say:

"As this candle burns, prosperity flows to me from all directions, in harmony with Divine Will, my own True Will, and with good to all."

4. Let the candle burn for a few minutes, then snuff it out—don't blow it out!

5. Repeat this ritual each day for eight days. Complete the spell on the day of the full moon.

Money Bath
rating: **silver**

This relaxing nighttime ritual puts you in the
mood to receive abundance.

Best times to perform this spell:

+ Begin eight days before the full moon

Ingredients or equipment needed:

+ A green ribbon
+ A few drops of Magick Money Massage Oil (see page 26)

1. Before going to bed, run a hot bath and pour a little
Magick Money Massage Oil in the water.

2. Tie the green ribbon around the bathtub faucet. As you
tie it, say aloud:

*"As this water flows and fills the tub, money flows
toward me and fills my life with abundance of all kinds."*

3. Soak in the bath water while you imagine all the good
things you desire coming to you and enriching your life—
enjoy your fantasies and make them as vivid as possible.

4. When you've finished, dry yourself and rub a little Magick
Money Massage Oil on your palms.

5. Repeat this ritual for eight consecutive nights, ending on
the night of the full moon. Perform this spell as often as you
like, to keep prosperity flowing your way.

Money Stones
rating: **silver**

For millennia, certain gemstones have been connected with wealth. Let these "money stones" bring you prosperity.

Best times to perform this spell:
- During the waxing moon
- Begin when the sun or moon is in Taurus
- On Thursdays

Ingredients or equipment needed:
- A piece of aventurine
- A piece of tiger's eye
- A piece of turquoise
- A piece of jade
- A piece of malachite
- A gold-colored freshwater pearl
- Magick Money Massage Oil (see page 26)
- A piece of gold silk cloth

1. Wash the stones with soap and water.

2. Dry them, then rub a little Magick Money Massage Oil on each stone.

3. Blow on the stones to infuse them with your breath, then wrap them in the gold cloth.

4. Place the gemstones in your purse, cash register, safe, or the Wealth Gua of your home to generate riches.

Unlimited Funds Spell

rating: **silver**

Write yourself a check to prime the pump
of unlimited prosperity.

Best times to perform this spell:
+ During the waxing moon
+ Begin when the sun or moon is in Taurus
+ On Thursdays

Ingredients or equipment needed:
+ A blank check
+ Magick Money Massage Oil (see page 26)

1. Write a check to yourself for any amount of money—but it should be an amount you can actually envision yourself receiving and accepting. (If you can't imagine a large sum, such as $1,000,000, start with something smaller, say $1,000.). Sign it "The Universe."

2. Put a drop of Magick Money Massage Oil on each corner of the check.

3. Carry the check in your wallet and look at it at least once every day to attract abundance. After you've received the amount of the check, burn the check and write yourself another for a larger sum. Repeat this spell as often as you like—the Bank of the Universe has unlimited funds.

Wealth Water Spell

rating: **silver**

Recently, Japanese researcher Masaru Emoto scientifically demonstrated the secrets behind this spell—but magicians have known for centuries that it really works.

Best times to perform this spell:

+ During the waxing moon
+ When the sun or moon is in Taurus
+ On Thursdays

Ingredients or equipment needed:

+ 8 ounces of spring water
+ A clear glass bottle
+ The 10 of diamonds or the 10 of pentacles from a tarot deck
+ A green silk cloth or pouch large enough to conceal the bottle

1. Wash the bottle, then pour the water into it.

2. Lay the card face up and set the bottle on it. Leave the bottle in place overnight, so the images on the card can be absorbed by the water.

3. In the morning, remove the card and conceal the bottle with the cloth or pouch (to hold the images in and prevent other images from interfering).

4. Drink a little of the water each day to attract abundance of all kinds.

Magick Mandala

Mandalas are beautiful, circular diagrams that represent the world. Use this ancient design to help you land the perfect job.

Best times to perform this spell:
+ During the waxing moon
+ On Thursdays or Sundays

Ingredients or equipment needed:
+ A large piece of paper or cardboard
+ Colored pens, markers, pencils, or crayons
+ Magazine pictures
+ A photo of you

1. Draw a circle on the paper or cardboard, then draw a horizontal line to divide it into two sectors. The part above the horizon represents the sky, ideas and ideals, the intellect, the spiritual dimensions of your goal. The part below the line symbolizes the earth, physical reality, practical matters, and the material factors involved in your objective.

2. Glue the photograph of yourself in the middle of the circle.

3. Next, draw designs, write affirmations, and/or paste pictures from magazines on the diagram to represent the job you desire and the benefits you intend to receive. In the bottom half, include images and words that suggest material perks or show the physical side of the job itself. In the top half, put images that describe the mental and/or spiritual aspects of the job.

4. Frame the finished mandala and hang it in a place where you will see it often.

Mask Magick

rating: **fog**

The power of suggestion makes this spell very powerful indeed. Remember how much you enjoyed "playing pretend" when you were a kid? Do it now to achieve success in your chosen field. Creative visualization and willpower—the essential ingredients in all magick—are what fuel this spell. The more you can involve your imagination, the better. The mask lets you transform your familiar identity and envision yourself in an entirely new way.

Best times to perform this spell:
+ Anytime

Ingredients or equipment needed:
+ A mask-making kit
+ Fabric, feathers, beads, glitter, lace, sequins, paint, etc.
+ Glue or paste

1. Acquire a mask-making kit from a crafts or hobby shop and follow the instructions for forming it to fit your face.

2. When the mask base has set, decorate it with symbols of the success you desire. Choose appropriate colors from Appendix A. Add pictures or objects that correspond to the job or goal you seek. Use your imagination and have fun!

3. Wear the mask often, gaze at your image in the mirror, and feel yourself becoming the person you desire to be.

Three Rs Spell

rating: **fog**

Recognition, rewards, and riches can be yours. Bay laurel leaves, linked with honor and success since ancient times, can help you attract fame and fortune.

Best times to perform this spell:

+ During the full moon

Ingredients or equipment needed:

+ 22 bay leaves
+ A needle and gold-colored thread

1. Fill a bathtub with hot water and add 22 bay leaves—22 is the number of power and leadership.

2. Soak in the hot water and imagine the greatness and glory signified by the bay leaves being absorbed into your skin.

3. When you've finished with your bath, remove the bay leaves and blot them dry.

4. Sew the leaves together to form a halo or crown and place it on your head.

5. Go outside and stand in the moonlight (weather permitting). Imagine the silver rays beaming down on you, as if you were a noted dignitary standing in a spotlight. Envision the three Rs—recognition, rewards, and riches—flowing toward you. Repeat this ritual on each full moon to ensure continued success.

Protection Spells

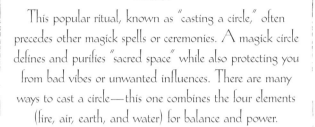

Magick Circle Ritual

rating: **silver**

This popular ritual, known as "casting a circle," often precedes other magick spells or ceremonies. A magick circle defines and purifies "sacred space" while also protecting you from bad vibes or unwanted influences. There are many ways to cast a circle—this one combines the four elements (fire, air, earth, and water) for balance and power.

Best times to perform this spell:
+ Anytime

Ingredients or equipment needed:
+ A bowl of water
+ A little sea salt
+ A stick of incense
+ Matches

1. Combine the salt and water.

2. Beginning at the easternmost point of the space in which you will be doing magick, walk in a clockwise circle, sprinkling drops of saltwater as you go, and say:

"With water and earth I cast this magick circle."

3. When you have completed the circle and returned to the east, light the incense. Again, walk in a clockwise circle, trailing incense smoke behind you, saying:

"With fire and air I cast this magick circle."

continued

4. Do whatever magick you choose within the circle. Remain inside until your spell is completed.

5. When you've finished, return to the east and hold your arm outstretched at your side. Walk in a counterclockwise circle and when you come back to the east, say aloud:

"This circle is now open."

House Protection Potion

rating: **silver**

Every happy home can benefit from a little magickal protection. This spell helps safeguard your living space and your belongings.

Best times to perform this spell:
+ During the waning moon
+ When the sun or moon is in Cancer
+ On Mondays

Ingredients or equipment needed:
+ A bunch of fresh basil
+ 2 quarts of water
+ 1 tsp. sea salt
+ A paintbrush

1. Heat the water in a large pot. Add the salt and basil. Simmer for about ten minutes. Pour the water through a sieve to remove the basil, then let the water cool.

2. Dip the brush in the basil-infused water and paint a penta-gram (a five-pointed star with a circle around it) on every door to your home to protect it against intruders or unwanted energies. While you are performing this ritual, repeat aloud:

> *"This magick potion protects my home and all my possessions, and keeps them safe at all times and in all situations."*

3. Dry the basil leaves, then crumble them and sprinkle them in the corners of your home. Bury them outside at the corners of your property, too.

Here's another way to protect your home and property.

Best times to perform this spell:

◆ During the waning moon

◆ When the sun or moon is in Cancer

◆ On Mondays

Ingredients or equipment needed:

◆ Sticks of rowan, ash, or pussy willow

◆ White string or ribbon

1. Cut thin sticks of rowan, ash, or pussy willow—each stick should be six inches long. (Ask the tree's permission first.) You'll need twice as many sticks as the number of windows and exterior doors in your home.

2. Tie two sticks together with the string or ribbon to form an X. Position one X above each exterior door and window in your home to safeguard your home from intruders. As you put each X in place, say aloud:

"This magick symbol protects my home and all my possessions, and keeps them safe at all times and in all situations."

3. When you've finished, envision a wall of pure white light surrounding your home and "sealing" each window and door.

Rune Amulet

rating: **silver**

Carry the amulet in your purse, pocket, or glove
compartment to keep you safe at all times.

Best times to perform this spell:

+ During the new moon
+ When the sun or moon is in Capricorn
+ On Saturdays

Ingredients or equipment needed:

+ A square piece of unfinished ash wood
+ A black felt-tip pen

1. Cut a piece of ash from a tree (remembering to first ask permission, and then to thank the tree) or purchase a small square of wood from a lumber yard. Sand it until it's smooth.

2. With the black felt-tip pen, draw one of these five runes—Thurisaz, Hagall, Fehu, Eihwaz, Eolh—in each corner of the ash square. Draw the fifth rune in the center of the square. (Consult a book of runes if you aren't familiar with these symbols.)

3. On the reverse side of the wood, write "I am protected at all times and in all situations." Carry the rune amulet with you to protect you wherever you go. (Note: If you're skilled at carving, you can engrave the runes on the wood. Hang the amulet on a chain to wear as a pendant.)

Clear the Air

rating: **silver**

Perform this spell to remove "bad vibes" from your home, office, or any other space.

Best times to perform this spell:

+ Anytime

Ingredients or equipment needed:

+ A sage smudge wand or a stick of sage incense

1. Light the sage wand or incense. Carry it through the area you wish to cleanse, allowing the smoke to waft behind you and clear the air.

Cat Protection Amulet

rating: **silver**

Cats' notorious curiosity often gets them into trouble. Attach this magick amulet to your cat's collar to keep him or her safe.

Best times to perform this spell:

* When the sun or moon is in Virgo
* On Wednesdays

Ingredients or equipment needed:

* A silver locket
* A small piece of bark from a pussy willow
* A small jade bead
* Amber essential oil
* A small square of white paper
* A pen with black ink

1. Write your cat's name on the piece of paper, then draw a star over the name and draw a circle around it.

2. Put a drop of amber essential oil on the paper.

3. Place the pussy willow bark and the jade bead on the paper and fold everything into a tiny packet, small enough to slip inside the locket.

4. Envision your pet completely enclosed in a ball of pure white light. Fasten the locket securely to your cat's collar while you repeat this affirmation three times:

"This magick amulet keeps [cat's name] safe and sound at all times and in all situations."

Note: While you're at it, get your cat a tag with your name and phone number on it and affix it to his/her collar, too.

Long-Distance Protection Spell

rating: **silver**

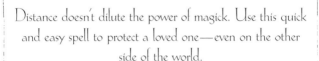

Distance doesn't dilute the power of magick. Use this quick and easy spell to protect a loved one—even on the other side of the world.

Best times to perform this spell:

✦ Anytime

1. Close your eyes and take a few deep breaths to calm and center yourself. Create a mental image of your loved one. Imagine this person wrapped in pure white light.

2. While you hold this picture in your mind, say aloud three times:

"[name] is protected by Divine White Light. S/he is safe and sound at all times and in all situations."

3. Repeat this spell as often as you wish. (Note: You can protect yourself this way, too.)

Pentagram Protection Spell

rating: **silver**

The pentagram or five-pointed star symbolizes the five points of the human body—head, arms, and legs. In magickal traditions, the pentagram is also a powerful protection emblem.

Best times to perform this spell:
+ Anytime

Ingredients or equipment needed:
+ A piece of white paper
+ Pens, pencils, or markers

1. With a black pen or marker, draw a star on the paper. Draw a circle around the star so it touches all five points and contains it.

2. Around the outside of the circle, write "[Name] is safe and sound at all times and in all situations." Decorate and embellish the pentagram, if you like, with images that suggest safety and protection to you.

3. Hang the finished picture on the door to your home or workplace to safeguard it. Or, fold the paper three times and put it in the glove compartment of your car to protect you while traveling. Carry the pentagram in your pocket or purse to shield you from harm. Give protection pentagrams to loved ones to keep them safe. Put a pentagram under your pillow to ward off bad dreams. You can also incorporate pentagrams into other protection amulets or spells.

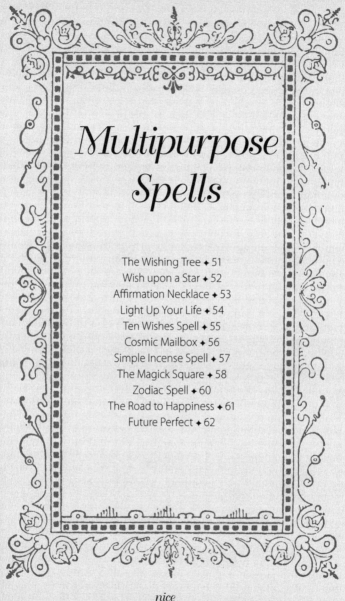

Multipurpose Spells

The Wishing Tree

rating: **silver**

The Druids considered trees to be sacred. This spell uses the tree's energy to empower your spell.

Best times to perform this spell:
+ Depends on your intentions—see Appendix D

Ingredients or equipment needed:
+ One or more ribbons

1. Choose a tree in your own yard or in the woods. Before you begin, ask the tree to assist you in making your wishes come true.

2. On a branch, tie a ribbon of a color that's appropriate to the nature of your wish (see Appendix A). As you tie the knot, say your wish aloud.

3. Make as many wishes as you like, using a different ribbon for each wish.

4. When you've finished, thank the tree.

Wish upon a Star

Stars are ancient symbols of hope—make five wishes come true with this easy spell.

Best times to perform this spell:

✦ Depends on your intentions—see Appendix D

Ingredients or equipment needed:

✦ A large sheet of paper or cardboard
✦ A marker, pen, or crayon

1. Draw a five-pointed star on the paper or cardboard—make it large enough so you can stand on the star.

2. On each of the star's rays, write a wish.

3. Stand in the center of the star and focus your thoughts on each of the rays individually, as you imagine each wish coming true.

4. When you've finished, step out of the star and store it in a safe place.

5. Repeat this spell as often as you like, updating the wishes as necessary.

Affirmation Necklace

rating: **silver**

This spell combines beauty with magick to bring you whatever your heart desires.

Best times to perform this spell:

+ Depends on your intention—see Appendix D

Ingredients or equipment needed:

+ Beads (see Appendices A and C)
+ Jeweler's wire

1. Affirmations are positive statements that express your wishes. Write a short statement that describes what you would like to achieve with your magick, such as "All my endeavors prosper."

2. Choose beads of a color or gemstone that relates to your wish, one for each letter in your affirmation. For example, you'd need twenty-one beads—perhaps jade or aventurine—for the above affirmation. Choose beads of a different color to separate the words.

3. String the beads so that they represent the words of your affirmation, with the contrasting beads in between to separate the words. In the example, you'd string three green beads together (ALL), then a few of a contrasting color, then two green beads (MY), a few more contrasting beads, nine green beads (ENDEAVORS), more contrasting beads, then seven green beads (PROSPER) to "spell out" the whole affirmation.

4. Add contrasting beads to make the necklace whatever length you want it to be. Wear the necklace as a magickal talisman to attract your desires.

Light Up Your Life

rating: **silver**

Did you know that blowing out candles on a birthday cake is a simple magick spell? Perform this variation with conscious intention to make all your wishes come true.

Best times to perform this spell:

+ Depends on your intentions—see Appendix D

Ingredients or equipment needed:

+ A cake
+ Candles in various colors
+ Matches

1. Bake (or buy) a cake. Choose a flavor that symbolizes your intentions—chocolate for love, spice for excitement, white for protection, golden-yellow for prosperity.

2. Put candles on the cake—as many as you like—in colors that correspond to your wishes (see Appendix A). Each candle represents a wish.

3. Light the candles and envision your dreams coming true. Hold these images in your mind while you blow out the candles with a single breath.

4. Eat the cake yourself or share it with others, especially those people who play roles in your intentions.

Ten Wishes Spell

rating: **fog**

The key to this spell's success is repetition. Do it every morning, faithfully, to make your fondest dreams come true.

Best times to perform this spell:

✦ Every morning

Ingredients or equipment needed:

✦ A piece of paper
✦ A pen or pencil
✦ Matches

1. Write ten wishes on a piece of paper. Make sure you word these wishes in the present tense and in a positive manner (for instance, "I now have plenty of money for everything I need and desire" instead of "I need money" or "I hope to be rich someday"). As you write down your requests, keep your mind focused on the end result you intend to bring about and imagine that the conditions you seek already exist—this is important.

2. When you've finished, read what you've written aloud.

3. Burn the paper in a fireplace, wood stove, barbecue grill, or other safe place.

4. Repeat this ritual every day. Each time one of your wishes is fulfilled, say "thank you," then replace it with another request.

Cosmic Mailbox

rating: **silver**

This spell petitions the deities (gods, goddesses, angels, spirits, ancestors) to help you accomplish your objectives or overcome problems.

Best times to perform this spell:

◆ Depends on your intentions—see Appendix D

Ingredients or equipment needed:

◆ Strips of paper
◆ Pen or pencil
◆ A cardboard box (any size) with a lid

1. Cut a slot in the lid of the box—this is your "cosmic mailbox." If you like, you can decorate the box with pictures that convey positive images.

2. Cut a strip of paper and on it write a wish, request, or problem with which you'd like a little help—as if you were writing a note to your favorite benevolent deity.

3. When you've finished, fold the piece of paper three times as you visualize your request being fulfilled.

4. Slip it into the box. Truly believe it will be taken care of in the proper time, in the correct way.

5. Repeat the process if you have more wishes or problems. Then stop worrying—doubt interferes with magick!

Simple Incense Spell

rating: **silver**

Incense is used to send messages to the higher realms—
perform this spell daily to communicate
with your favorite deities.

Best times to perform this spell:

+ Every day

Ingredients or equipment needed:

+ Stick, cone, coil, or loose incense
+ An incense burner
+ Matches

1. Calm and center yourself.

2. Light incense in a fireproof incense burner. If you know feng shui, place the incense in the sector of your home that corresponds to your wishes.

3. Watch the smoke and focus your mind on your wishes, intentions, or requests, while you say aloud:

"As this smoke rises to the heavens carrying my prayers to you, [Favorite Deity], please manifest these requests in my life now, in harmony with Divine Will, my own True Will, and with good to all."

The Magick Square

This special combination of numbers and gemstones helps your wishes magickally materialize.

Best times to perform this spell:

+ The Equinoxes and Solstices

Ingredients or equipment needed:

+ 9 gemstones
+ A black cloth
+ The Magick Square grid below

4	9	2
3	5	7
8	1	6

1. Redraw a larger version of the Magick Square shown here and lay it face up on a table. (Notice that when you add the numbers in the squares horizontally, vertically, or diagonally they total 15.)

2. In each square, write a wish.

3. Place gemstones that relate to your wishes (see Appendix C) in the corresponding squares, one stone per square.

4. Cover the square and stones with the black cloth. Leave the cover in place overnight.

5. In the morning, remove the cloth and stones, store them in a safe place for future use, then burn the square to release your wishes into the cosmos.

Zodiac Spell

rating: **depends on your intentions**

On your birthday, make twelve wishes to attract good
fortune into every area of your life.

Best times to perform this spell:
+ The morning of your birthday

Ingredients or equipment needed:
+ A tarot deck
+ A large sheet of paper
+ A pen or pencil

1. On the piece of paper, draw a circle about two feet in
diameter, then divide it into twelve equal sections so it looks
like a pie with twelve slices. What you've drawn is a blank
horoscope chart—the twelve sectors known as "houses" represent twelve areas of your life (see Appendix G).

2. Choose twelve cards from a tarot deck—the cards should
describe what you want to bring into each related area of
your life (see Appendix F).

3. Put one card in each house, beginning with the first
house, located at the 8:00-to-9:00 position on a clock's face.
Continue in counterclockwise direction until you have laid all
twelve cards on the wheel.

4. Leave the cards in place until the next morning, then
remove them and put them back in the deck. Save the blank
wheel for next year.

The Road to Happiness
rating: **silver**

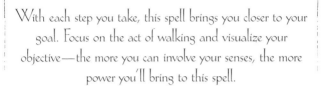

With each step you take, this spell brings you closer to your goal. Focus on the act of walking and visualize your objective—the more you can involve your senses, the more power you'll bring to this spell.

Best times to perform this spell:
+ Depends on your intentions—see Appendix D

Ingredients or equipment needed:
+ Permanent markers
+ Shoes

1. Choose permanent markers in colors that correspond to your objectives (see Appendix A).

2. Write your wishes—as many as you like—on the soles of your shoes.

3. As you walk, envision your dreams coming true. Chant your wishes aloud as you walk. As you utter a wish, picture the corresponding end result you desire or a symbol that vividly represents it. For instance, every time you say the word "wealth" see yourself picking up $100 bills and stuffing them in your pocket. Don't let your mind wander—keep your attention on your objectives! Each step brings you nearer to happiness, love, health, prosperity, success, and all the things you desire.

Future Perfect

rating: **depends on your intentions**

This spell uses feng shui's magick to help you create your ideal future.

Best times to perform this spell:

+ Depends on your intentions—see Appendix D

Ingredients or equipment needed:

+ 3 objects that symbolize the future you desire
+ A sage smudge wand or sage incense
+ Matches

1. Stand at the door you use most often to enter or leave your home and face inside. Imagine a straight line between you and the furthest point in your living space (let your mind project through walls or other obstructions).

2. Go to this spot, light a sage smudge wand or sage incense, and let the smoke waft into the air to clear away any ambient energies.

3. Place three objects here to represent the future you desire—a wedding ring, for instance, symbolizes marriage; a silver dollar signifies wealth.

4. Gaze at these items for a few minutes while you visualize the conditions they represent manifesting in your life.

5. Each day, move these three objects around a bit (to keep their energies activated) while you focus on attracting whatever they symbolize.

6. As soon as a situation you've imagined materializes, remove the respective object and replace it with something else.

Miscellaneous Spells

nice

Reading Tea Leaves

rating: **fog**

This time-honored practice lets you tap your intuition to gain insights and guidance. The aromatherapy properties of peppermint and lemon help to clear your mind and stimulate your awareness.

Best times to perform this spell:

◆ Anytime

Ingredients or equipment needed:

◆ 1 cup spring water
◆ Loose peppermint herbal tea
◆ A perforated tea ball or spoon
◆ A few drops of lemon juice
◆ A plain cup or mug (no decorations)

1. Fill a tea ball with loose tea and place it in a cup or mug (clear glass or white is best).

2. Heat the water, then pour it over the tea ball and let it steep for a few minutes.

3. Add a few drops of lemon juice.

4. Sip the tea while you relax and center yourself—try to keep your mind free of random thoughts.

continued

5. When you've finished drinking the tea, empty some of the wet tea leaves into the bottom of the cup and swirl them around (if necessary, add a few drops of water).

6. Gaze into the cup—what does the pattern formed by the tea leaves make you think of? Pay attention to the first ideas or impressions that pop into your mind, without censoring yourself.

Winter Solstice Good Luck Charm

rating: **silver**

Give this special holiday talisman to friends and loved ones to bring them blessings throughout the New Year.

Best times to perform this spell:

+ The Winter Solstice

Ingredients or equipment needed:

+ An oak "Yule" log
+ Small cloth pouches, one for each person
+ Ribbons, one for each person
+ Pink rose petals
+ Acorns
+ Cedar chips
+ Chamomile or lavender flowers
+ Strips of paper
+ A pen or marker

1. On the eve of the Winter Solstice (also known as Yule), burn an oak log in a fireplace or wood stove.

2. In the morning, collect the ashes and put some in each pouch.

3. Add a rose petal (for love), an acorn (for strength), a chip of cedar (for prosperity), and a few chamomile or lavender buds (for serenity) to each pouch.

4. Write a special blessing or wish for each person on a strip of paper.

continued

5. Fold the paper three times and slip it into the pouch.

6. Close the pouches with the ribbons and, as you tie three knots, repeat your New Year's wish for each of your loved ones.

Spell to Contact a Departed Loved One

rating: **fog**

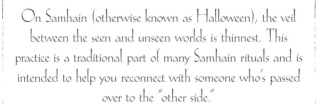

On Samhain (otherwise known as Halloween), the veil between the seen and unseen worlds is thinnest. This practice is a traditional part of many Samhain rituals and is intended to help you reconnect with someone who's passed over to the "other side."

Best times to perform this spell:

+ Samhain eve (October 31)

Ingredients or equipment needed:

+ A votive candle in a fireproof holder
+ Matches

1. Light the candle and set it in a safe place.

2. Sit or stand and gaze into the flame, while you think about the person with whom you wish to communicate. Keep an open heart and an open mind.

3. Allow your intuition to reach "through the veil" into the nonphysical realms. Send thoughts, messages, and prayers to your loved one on the other side.

4. Listen carefully and pay attention to any feelings or impressions you receive—your loved one may be trying to contact you, too.

5. When you've finished, extinguish the candle.

Peaceful Family Gathering Potion

rating: **silver**

Even the happiest family get-togethers can be emotionally charged events. Spray a little of this magickal mist into the air to reduce stress.

Best times to perform this spell:

✦ 24 hours before a family gathering

Ingredients or equipment needed:

✦ A clear spray bottle
✦ 6 ounces of spring water
✦ A few drops essential oil of lavender
✦ A small amethyst
✦ A blank label (or 2" x 4" piece of paper)
✦ A blue pen or marker
✦ A dark cloth

1. Draw a peace sign or write the word "PEACE" on the label and affix it to the bottle, so that the word or symbol faces in.

2. Pour the spring water into the bottle, then add the lavender essential oil and the amethyst.

3. Shake the bottle three times to "charge" it.

4. Cover the bottle with the cloth overnight.

5. Before your relatives arrive, remove the cloth and spray this magick potion around the area where the gathering will take place.

6. Envision the space filled with pure white light. If necessary, mist the area again periodically to dispel tension and encourage serenity.

Pain, Pain Go Away

rating: **silver**

When you're plagued by painful emotions—fear, jealousy, anger, anxiety, abandonment—this technique helps diminish their power over you.

Best times to perform this spell:

✦ Anytime

Ingredients or equipment needed:

✦ Rescue Remedy flower essence (see Appendix H)

1. Put two drops of Rescue Remedy under your tongue.

2. Close your eyes and concentrate on taking slow, deep breaths. As you inhale, allow yourself to fully experience the painful feelings—don't try to block or avoid them. If you wish, envision them as something unsavory, such as filthy smoke or a foul odor.

3. As you exhale, visualize these painful emotions being broken up and dispersed into the vastness of a clear, blue sky.

4. Think the words:

"I am free of fear, the source of all pain."

5. Concentrate on your breathing and allow it to relax your body. Continue this focused, rhythmic breathing until the pain decreases and you feel calmer.

Lucky Letter Spell

rating: **silver**

Send good luck to a total stranger with this easy spell.
According to many magickal and spiritual traditions,
whatever thoughts and energies you send out return to you
threefold, so this spell benefits you, too.

Best times to perform this spell:

+ Anytime

Ingredients or equipment needed:

+ Paper
+ Pen
+ A library book

1. Write an anonymous "letter" to someone, wishing him or her good luck.

2. Take the letter to your local library and slip it into a book, then place the book back on the shelf. The next person who reads the book will receive your blessings.

Let Peace Prevail

rating: **silver**

Is there "bad blood" between you and another person?
This spell can help dissolve unpleasant feelings and
restore peace.

Best times to perform this spell:
◆ Anytime

Ingredients or equipment needed:
◆ Paper and pen
◆ A white ribbon

1. Write a letter to the person with whom you are having
problems. Explain your side in a pleasant, non-threatening
way, without making any judgments or accusations. Also
apologize for any bad behavior or unkind thoughts and
words on your part. Express your desire to rectify the situation and put this matter behind you. At the end of the letter,
write

*"May peace, love, and acceptance exist between us, now
and always. Blessed Be."*

Sign your name.

2. Roll the paper into a scroll and tie it with the white ribbon.

3. Burn the scroll to release peaceful vibrations into the cosmos. (Note: This is a good way to make peace with someone
who is no longer living on the earth plane or someone you
can't communicate with via ordinary channels.)

Pendulum Magick

rating: **fog**

Looking for answers to baffling questions? Need a little guidance? A pendulum may be just the tool for you.

Best times to perform this spell:

+ Anytime

Ingredients or equipment needed:

+ A locket with a chain or ready-made pendulum with a chamber for "loading"

1. Calm and center yourself. Place a small amount of a substance that corresponds to your question or concern (such as a lover's hair) inside the locket or pendulum's compartment.

2. Loosely hold the locket or pendulum by the chain, so that it dangles a few inches above a tabletop.

3. Ask a question and wait patiently until the pendulum starts to move of its own accord—don't move it yourself intentionally. If the pendulum swings from side to side, the answer is "no." If it swings back and forth (toward you, then away from you), the answer is "yes." If it swings in a clockwise circle, the situation is favorable. If it circles in a counterclockwise direction, the situation is unfavorable.

4. Work with your pendulum regularly and you'll find it quickly responds to your queries, offering insights and guidance into the past, present, and future.

Relocation Spell

rating: **fog**

Moving can be a stressful experience—this spell facilitates the process and helps you relocate to a place that's right for you.

Best times to perform this spell:
+ When the sun or moon is in Cancer
+ On Mondays

Ingredients or equipment needed:
+ A plant
+ A shovel
+ Water

1. Acquire a potted plant that represents you. Be sure to choose something that is well-suited to living outdoors in the area where you plan to relocate.

2. Take the plant to the place where you will be living, dig a hole, and nestle it in the ground.

3. Water the plant and send it loving thoughts. Tell the plant to put down roots, so that it—and you—will thrive in this new place.

4. Sit beside the plant and close your eyes. Establish an energetic connection with the plant. Imagine yourself also "putting down roots" and growing strong and healthy in this new location.

5. Visit the plant often. Continue to care for it—water and fertilize it, trim its leaves, etc. If you like, you can tie ribbons on it or add a few drops of Rescue Remedy to the water. Remember, the attention and love you lavish on the plant symbolize the emotional support and nourishment you are giving yourself during this time of transition.

Fire and Water Energizing Ritual

rating: **silver**

Whenever you need a quick energy boost, take a few minutes to perform this revitalizing spell.

Best times to perform this spell:

+ Anytime

1. Sit in a quiet place where you won't be disturbed—the best spot is outdoors near a body of water.

2. Close your eyes, begin breathing slowly and deeply as you relax and center yourself.

3. Imagine your spine is a tree trunk sending its roots deep, down into the earth's center.

4. Envision water (in the form of blue-green light) being drawn by these roots up through the base of your spine, into your body. See and feel the water flowing up your spine, through your chakras, cleansing, calming, and nourishing you. Imagine it spouting out the top of your head like a fountain and washing down over your body. Do this at least three times.

5. Visualize the sun's golden rays shining down on you and entering a portal in the top of your head. Sense these rays clearing away impurities and warming your body all the way down to the tips of your toes. Feel your breath mixing with the sunlight and swirling through your body to energize every cell. Continue this visualization for a few minutes, until you feel rejuvenated.

Ritual to Break an Old Habit

rating: **fog**

Is an old habit, attitude, or behavior holding you back? Perform this ritual to help break its power over you.

Best times to perform this spell:

✦ A few days before the new moon
✦ When the sun or moon is in Scorpio

Ingredients or equipment needed:

✦ A symbol of the habit you wish to eliminate
✦ A black cloth
✦ A shovel
✦ A large stone

1. Calm and center yourself. Envision a cloud of pure white light surrounding and infusing you with its cleansing energy.

2. Wrap the symbol of your old habit—a pack of cigarettes, a beer bottle, a lottery ticket, a donut—in the black cloth.

3. Then take it to a spot near a cemetery, dig a hole, and bury the object. Cover it up and place the stone over it. The image of the cemetery reinforces your intention to "kill" the unwanted habit. Say aloud,

> *"I'm no longer in your grasp.*
> *I am free of you at last."*

4. Repeat this ritual (if necessary) before each new moon, until you've completely eliminated the unwanted habit.

Sweet Dreams Potion

rating: **silver**

This sweet spell combines scent with sound to promote pleasant dreams.

Best times to perform this spell:

+ Anytime

Ingredients or equipment needed:

+ 8 ounces of spring water
+ Chamomile tea
+ 2 drops lavender essential oil
+ 2 drops vanilla essential oil
+ A small tumbled amethyst
+ A spray bottle
+ A bell

1. Brew a cup of hot chamomile tea.

2. Let the tea cool, then pour it into the spray bottle. Add the essential oils and the amethyst.

3. Shake the mixture three times to "charge" it.

4. Before retiring for the night, ring the bell over your bed three times to chase away any disruptive or unbalanced energies.

5. Mist your pillow lightly with the potion to encourage sweet dreams and restful sleep.

Spirit Animal Assistance

rating: **fog**

Shamans often invoke the assistance of spirit or "totem" animals. You, too, can draw on the abilities of animal guides to enhance your own power.

Best times to perform this spell:

◆ Anytime

Ingredients or equipment needed:

◆ A statuette of the animal you wish to emulate

1. Think of an animal that possesses qualities you desire. For example, elephants are incredibly strong, eagles are known for their keen vision, dogs are loyal, tigers are fierce and fearless.

2. Find a small statuette of this animal.

3. Calm and center yourself, while you hold the figurine in your hand. Ask the animal to imbue you with its strength, patience, gentleness, wisdom, courage, etc. so that you may be better equipped to deal with whatever challenge is facing you.

4. Act out behavior that's characteristic of the animal— roar like a lion or walk as slow as a turtle, for instance. Imagine the qualities you desire becoming part of your own nature—you might even sense yourself merging with the animal temporarily. Invite your animal helper to visit you in your dreams.

5. Display the statuette where you will see it often and touch it whenever you seek its assistance. Note: Remember to thank the animal for helping you.

What Colors Should You Use in Magick Spells?

Colors play a part in many magick spells. Keep these color correspondences in mind when you are using candles, ribbons or cords, "mojo" bags, clothing, or images in your spells.

Use This Color	If Your Spell Involves
red	passion, vitality, courage
orange	energy, action, enthusiasm, confidence, expansion
yellow	creativity, optimism, happiness
green	healing, growth, fertility, prosperity
light blue	purity, serenity, mental clarity, relief from pain
royal blue	loyalty, insight, inspiration, independence
indigo	intuition, mental focus, inducing visions
purple	wisdom, spirituality, power
white	purity, clearing, wholeness, protection
black	power, banishing, setting boundaries
pink	love, friendship, affection, joy, self-love
brown	grounding, permanence, stability

Appendix B
Magickal Plants

Because they are living entities, plants possess magickal powers that can help you in spellworking. For centuries, wise men and women have prepared botanical charms, lotions, potions, and remedies for every imaginable purpose. Here are just a few you may want to try. (**Note**: Some of these plants are poisonous, can irritate the skin, or produce allergic reactions, so use with care.)

If This Is Your Intention	Use These Plants
love	rose, jasmine, red clover, myrtle, orchid, ylang-ylang, peach, apple, raspberry, strawberry, passion flower
prosperity	pine, cedar, mint, sunflower, sandalwood, marigold, parsley, moneyplant, saffron, asparagus
protection	basil, fennel, sage, ash, peony, snapdragon, verbena, pussy willow, fern, star anise, rowan, garlic
intuition/insight	narcissus, lavender, wisteria, ginger, lily of the valley, lotus
purification	sage, pine, rosemary, aloe
peace of mind	lemon balm, lavender, iris, chamomile
courage/strength	pepper, gentian, loosestrife, beech, pine, oak, mustard, chives, ivy

Appendix C
What Gemstones Should You Use in Magick Spells?

Long before they were prized for their monetary value, gemstones were used in magickal amulets and talismans.

If This Is Your Intention	Use These Stones
love/friendship	rose quartz, coral, opal, diamond, emerald, pearl, peridot
prosperity	aventurine, jade, tiger's eye, turquoise, star sapphire
protection	amber, jade, malachite, tourmaline
healing	jade, jasper, agate, bloodstone, amber, pearl
intuition/insight	amethyst, lapis lazuli, moonstone, opal, aquamarine, sapphire, pearl
stability/grounding	onyx, hematite, jet, obsidian, smoky quartz
courage/vitality	carnelian, ruby, topaz, garnet, diamond, bloodstone
career success/fame	ruby, topaz, garnet, diamond, sapphire, aventurine
to enhance any spell	clear quartz crystal

nice

Appendix D
When Should You Do Magick Spells?

Day	Planetary Ruler	Do Magick Spells For
Sunday	Sun	creativity, leadership, fame
Monday	Moon	home, family, intuition, fertility
Tuesday	Mars	sports, vitality, action, sex, men
Wednesday	Mercury	communication, intellect, travel
Thursday	Jupiter	growth, luck, travel, prosperity
Friday	Venus	love, joint ventures, women
Saturday	Saturn	limits, reduction, permanence

Moon Phase	Do Magick Spells For
New moon	beginnings
Waxing moon	growth, attraction, increase
Full moon	recognition, rewards, completion, clarity, fulfillment
Waning moon	reduction, endings

When the Sun or Moon Is In	Do Magick Spells That Involve
Aries	courage, sex, men, sports, vitality, action, beginnings
Taurus	prosperity, fertility, creativity, love, sex, property, gardening
Gemini	short trips, mental pursuits, education, neighbors, siblings
Cancer	home, protection, family, children, women
Leo	career success, fame, creativity, leadership, games of chance
Virgo	health, job-related matters, coworkers, pets
Libra	love, creativity, legal issues, social standing, peace
Scorpio	power, sex, insight/intuition, investments, other people's money, transformation, overcoming obstacles
Sagittarius	long-distance travel, growth, spiritual matters, education
Capricorn	business, stability, protection, financial security, endings, boundaries, banishing
Aquarius	friends, groups, change, insight
Pisces	creativity, intuition, dreams or visions, ocean voyages, endings

Appendix E
What Numbers Should You Use in Magick Spells?

In our everyday world, numbers help us count and quantify, but in the world of magick, numbers have deeper, symbolic meanings. In some occult traditions, numbers were used in esoteric texts to convey secret knowledge. Many spells draw on the hidden significance of numbers—keep the following meanings in mind when you are tying knots, lighting candles, deciding how many ingredients to put into a talisman, etc.

Number	Secret Meaning
1	beginnings, individuality, focused energy
2	partnerships, joint ventures, union of opposites, balance
3	change, creativity, action/activation
4	stability, form, material goods
5	dispersion, instability, movement, communication
6	give and take, cooperation, fertility
7	inner peace, wholeness, development, contemplation
8	manifestation, wealth, work, permanence
9	growth, fulfillment, fortune, transitions, endings
0	unity, wholeness, completion, protection

What Cards Should You Use in Magick Spells?

The vivid images on tarot cards can be used in magick spells to focus your mind and produce results. If you don't own a tarot deck, you can substitute cards from a regular playing deck.

If This Is Your Intention	Use These Cards
love	The Lovers, Ace of Cups, Ace of Wands, 2 of Cups, 6 of Cups, 10 of Cups, Ace of Hearts, 10 of Hearts, Queen of Hearts
prosperity	Emperor, Ace of Pentacles, 9 of Pentacles, 10 of Pentacles, Queen of Pentacles, King of Pentacles, Ace of Diamonds, 9 of Diamonds, 10 of Diamonds, Queen of Diamonds, King of Diamonds
protection/ security	Strength, 9 of Wands, 9 of Clubs
good luck	Wheel of Fortune, The Star, 9 of Cups, 9 of Hearts
intuition/ insight	High Priestess, The Moon, The Sun, The Magician, Queen of Hearts
health/vitality	Strength, The Sun, King of Clubs
career success/fame	Emperor, Empress, The Sun, King of Wands, Queen of Wands, King of Clubs, Queen of Clubs

If This Is Your Intention	Use These Cards
victory/achievement	The Chariot, The World, 6 of Wands, 6 of Clubs
travel/adventure	The Fool, Knight of Wands, Joker, Jack of Clubs
domestic happiness	4 of Wands, 4 of Clubs
legal matters	Justice, Hierophant
peace of mind	Temperance, The World, The Hermit, Strength
power	The Magician, The Emperor, The Empress
intellect/communication	King of Swords, Queen of Swords, Ace of Swords, King of Spades, Queen of Spades, Ace of Spades
creativity	High Priestess, Empress, Queen of Wands, Ace of Wands, Queen of Hearts, Ace of Hearts

Appendix G
Astrology and Magick

Astrology plays a role in many magick spells and rituals. Birthstones, for instance, are gems that resonate with the vibrations of the zodiac signs. Performing spells during certain moon phases can enhance their power. The lists below show the areas of life that correspond to the twelve signs of the zodiac and the twelve houses of a birth chart.

Zodiac Sign	Correspondences
Aries	men, sports, conflict, vitality, action, beginnings
Taurus	money, gardening, art, music, fertility, sensuality
Gemini	communication, short trips, mental pursuits
Cancer	home, family, children, women, real estate
Leo	self-expression, leadership, leisure, games of chance, love affairs
Virgo	health, work, coworkers, pets
Libra	partnerships, legal issues, art, socializing, beauty
Scorpio	hidden matters, investments, other people's money, transformation, sex, the occult
Sagittarius	long-distance travel, higher education, religion
Capricorn	business, authority figures, structure, elders, boundaries
Aquarius	friends, groups, technology, change, the future
Pisces	intuition, liquids, sleep, imagination, music, poetry

Horoscope House	Area of Life
First	self, identity, physical appearance, the body
Second	personal resources, money, physical abilities
Third	siblings, neighbors, early education, short trips
Fourth	home, family, childhood, security, core issues
Fifth	creativity, love affairs, pleasure
Sixth	work, coworkers, service, health matters
Seventh	partners (love or business), agents, advisors
Eighth	partner's money/resources, hidden abilities
Ninth	spirituality, higher knowledge, long trips, the law
Tenth	career, public image
Eleventh	friends, group activities, ideologies
Twelfth	hidden fears, innate talents, secrets, intuition

Appendix H
Resources

Essential and Massage Oils

Aromaland
800-933-5267
www.aromaland.com

Aura Cacia
800-437-3301
www.auracacia.com

Good Clean Fun
541-344-4483
www.sacredmomentsproducts.com

Sun's Eye
800-786-7393
www.sunseye.com

Skye Botanicals
800-666-2225
www.skyebotanicals.com

V'Tae
800-643-3001
www.vtae.com

Flower Remedies

Flower Essence Society
P.O. Box 1769
Nevada City, CA 95959
www.flowersociety.org

Nelson Bach, USA
Wilmington, MA 01887

Sage and Smudging Products

Spirit Dancer Sage
800-SAGE-007

Light Stones
800-82-PEACE

Gemstones and Crystals

Heaven and Earth
800-942-9423

Craftstones
760-789-1620
www.craftstones.com

Energy Stones
866-312-0829
www.energystones.com

Wegner Crystal Mines
800-367-9888
www.wegnercrystalmines.com

Tarot Cards

U.S. Games Systems
800-544-2637
www.usgamesinc.com

Llewellyn Publications
800-THE-MOON
www.llewellyn.com

Specialty Candles

Lunar Cycle Candles
530-546-5470

Coventry Candles
800-810-3837

Sweet Spirit Candles
888-871-9001
www.sweetspiritcandles.com

Shadow and Light
800-997-4236
www.shadowandlightinc.com

Bennington Candles
888-314-3003

Aromaland
800-933-5267
www.aromaland.com

Incense

Shoyeido
800-786-5476
www.shoyeido.com

Ravenwood
800-777-5021
www.ravenwoodspa.com

DharmaCrafts
800-794-9862
www.dharmacrafts.com

Aromaland
800-933-5267
www.aromaland.com

Magick Wands

Crystal Visions Wands
800-339-5106
www.highvibes.org

Willowroot
800-554-0113
www.realmagicwands.com

Water/Wind/Stone
505-424-9020
www.waterwindstone.com

Seeds of Light
800-378-4327
www.dreamseeds.com

Magical Delights
888-317-0887
www.magicaldelights.com

JC Enterprises
800-814-6330

Pendulums

Silver Streak
800-526-9990
www.silverstreakind.com

Crystal Courier Imports
800-397-1863
www.crystalcourier.com

Life Designs
888-773-8003

Cauldrons

Sumitra
800-728-4468
www.sumitragifts.com

Drums

Rhythm Fusion
831-426-7975
www.rhythmfusion.com

Mamadou
www.mamadou.com

About the Author

Skye Alexander is the author of more than twenty fiction and nonfiction books, most of them on magick, tarot, astrology, feng shui, and other metaphysical subjects. Her first novel *Hidden Agenda* won the Kiss of Death Award for best book of romantic suspense and her short stories have been published in numerous anthologies. A practitioner of the occult arts for more than two decades, she appeared in a Discovery Channel TV special performing a ritual at Stonehenge. She lives in Texas with her feline familiar, Domino (*www.skyealexander.com*).

naughty
or
nice?

you decide . . .

Naughty

Spells

Sexy & Scandalous

Skye Alexander

A
Adams Media
Avon, Massachusetts

Published by Adams Media, an F+W Publications Company
57 Littlefield Street
Avon, MA 02322
www.adamsmedia.com

ISBN: 1-59337-631-6
Printed in Canada

J I H G F E D C B A

Library of Congress Cataloging-in-Publication Data

Alexander, Skye.
Naughty spells/nice spells / Skye Alexander.
p.   cm.
ISBN 1-59337-631-6
1. Magic. 2. Charms. I. Title.
BF1611.A445 2006
133.4'4--dc22
2006013594

This publication is designed to provide accurate and authoritative information with regard to the subject matter covered. It is sold with the understanding that the publisher is not engaged in rendering legal, accounting, or other professional advice. If legal advice or other expert assistance is required, the services of a competent professional person should be sought.

> —From a *Declaration of Principles* jointly adopted by a Committee of the American Bar Association and a Committee of Publishers and Associations

Many of the designations used by manufacturers and sellers to distinguish their product are claimed as trademarks. Where those designations appear in this book and Adams Media was aware of a trademark claim, the designations have been printed with initial capital letters.

Interior art © Dover Publications.

This book is available at quantity discounts for bulk purchases. For information, please call 1-800-872-5627.

To R.L., who shared his magick l with me

contents

𝔐iscellaneous 𝔖pells 65

Introduction

What Is Magick?

According to Aleister Crowley, one of magick's most notorious bad boys, "Every intentional act is a magical act." Basically, this means that whenever you set a goal for yourself, then focus your willpower toward achieving your goal, you activate energy and begin shaping it to suit your purposes. Energy, as you know, is the raw material that makes up our Universe. By molding energy, you literally create your own reality.

Magick is all in the mind. Before something can materialize in the physical world, somebody first has to imagine it. An architect envisions a house before it can be built. You do the same thing when you perform magick—you create a mental image of the result you intend to produce, then fuel it with your will and emotions. Of course, to build a house you need hammers, saws, and other tools. In magick, spells are the tools you use to fabricate your wishes.

Underlying all magick is a simple physics principle: Every action produces a reaction. Remember that old computer axiom, garbage in, garbage out? Magick is like that, too: If you put bad thoughts and feelings in, you'll get bad stuff out. And vice versa. So, be careful what you ask for!

Magick Isn't Just Black and White

When another driver cuts you off or grabs your parking space do you rattle off a string of colorful curses? When your boss dumps a rush project on your desk at 4:57 Friday evening, do you imagine all sorts of nasty things happening to him during the weekend? If so, you're performing black magick!

People usually associate black magick with wicked witches and wayward wizards—and to be sure, conniving conjurers like that do exist. But most black magick is performed by ordinary men and women who don't even realize they're doing it.

Magick can be broken down into three categories: black, white, and gray. Not surprisingly, the gray areas are the sticky ones. Although some magicians might quibble with my definitions, here's a simple explanation of the three types.

- ✦ Black magick means anything done to harm someone else.
- ✦ White magick is done to obtain higher knowledge, evolve spiritually, or strengthen your connection with the Source.
- ✦ Gray magick includes everything else.

As you can see, most magick—including the spells in this book—falls into the gray area.

Shades of Gray

Let's get one thing straight—there's nothing wrong with doing magick to get what you want. In fact, that's the reason most of us perform spells. You can use magick just as you use your talents to improve your lot in life. But if you injure someone else in order to achieve your own objectives, you're crossing the line from gray to black magick.

Wicca, the spiritual path many modern-day Western witches follow, puts it concisely: "Do what you will, but harm none." Now that seems plain enough, doesn't it? A spell designed to kill your business partner so you get total control of the company and your joint assets obviously falls into the black category. A spell to steal your sister's husband? Black again.

But what about doing magick to get a job that your best friend also wants? Or to win the heart of that really cute guy you met at a party Saturday night (the one who didn't ask for your phone number)? Now we're talking shades of gray.

Some spells fall at the "silver" end of the spectrum, others at the "nimbus" end. But sometimes it's kind of hard to tell. Even well-intended spells may infringe on another person's free will. Believe me, I've been there, done that. And most witches, if they're honest, will admit they have too.

Here's an example. Let's say your brother is sick and you decide to do a spell to heal him. Sounds like a positive use of magick, right? Well, maybe yes, maybe no. Perhaps your brother has been pushing himself too hard and needs a rest big-time, but the only way his body can get him to slow down is to send him to bed with the flu. His illness is actually serving a good purpose; therefore, doing a get-well spell could be interfering with his body's natural protective processes. See what I mean about gray areas?

Many spells are considered "bad" because they're manipulative. Let's talk some more about that cute guy from the party. And let's say you know for a fact he's not involved with anyone else. Isn't it okay to go for it? Again, the answer is maybe. In situations like this, you need to ask yourself a couple of questions. One, if he isn't interested in you, are you interfering with his own free will by doing a spell to snag him? Two, do you really want someone who's not that into you or would you be better off with someone else?

Okay, I admit, this is a toughy. Love spells are the ones people most often misuse. The best way to handle this dilemma is to add a "disclaimer" at the end of your spell, something like "if this is for our highest good." This allows the Universe to make the final decision and take responsibility for the outcome. You're off the hook—if the relationship isn't right, it won't happen. An even better approach is to do a spell to attract a partner who is right for you in every way. Don't specify who that might be, let the Universe send you the perfect lover.

How can you decide if the spell you're doing is naughty or nice? Consider the possible consequences—are you willing to accept what happens? Would you advise your best friend to do it? How would you react if someone did it to you? Trust your feelings—if you don't feel right about it, don't do it.

Using the Spells in This Book

The spells in this book fall into the "gray area." Some are nice; some are just a bit naughty. To warn you ahead of time, I've done what the motion picture industry does with films—I've rated the spells according to a "grayscale" standard.

- ✦ silver = nice and safe
- ✦ fog = not usually harmful, but maybe a little murky
- ✦ smoky = where there's smoke, there may be fire; use caution
- ✦ nimbus = like dark clouds, these can lead to stormy conditions; proceed at your own risk

Often, your intention is the only difference between one category and the next. The way you word a spell can shift it from fog to smoky or even nimbus. Some spells are ranked darker because they are potentially more powerful and require more skill. Others, like X-rated films, get a nimbus rating due to their sexual content.

Before you do a dark spell, consider whether you can produce the same result using a slightly lighter touch. I'm not saying you should avoid the smoky or nimbus spells—they can be very powerful and exciting—but they do involve more risk and aren't for beginners. Remember, the choice is always yours.

Love Spells

The Beat Goes On

This spell can increase the love in an existing relationship or rekindle the fire between you and a former flame.

Best times to perform this spell:
+ During the waxing moon
+ When either the sun or moon is in Taurus or Libra
+ On Tuesdays or Fridays

Ingredients or equipment needed:
+ A drum
+ A small cloth or leather pouch
+ A photo of the person you desire and a photo of yourself or a photo of you both together
+ Essential oil of rose, ylang-ylang, jasmine, or musk
+ A piece of parchment (or good quality paper)
+ A pen with red ink

1. On the piece of parchment, write "[partner's name] and I are lovers and we are very happy together," then fold it three times.

2. Lay the photos face to face and fold them together (or, if the photo shows both of you together, just fold it) so they fit into the pouch.

3. Dab essential oil on the photo(s) and the parchment.

4. Slip the pictures and parchment into the pouch, then fasten the pouch to the drum.

5. Play the drum regularly, while holding your wish in your mind. Each time you strike the drum you send your intention out into the Universe, where it will be acted upon and brought into physical reality.

Lovers' Knot

rating: **smoky**

This powerful spell strengthens the bond
between you and your beloved.

Best times to perform this spell:

+ The full moon
+ When either the sun or moon is in Taurus or Libra
+ On Fridays

Ingredients or equipment needed:

+ One of your hairs
+ One of your beloved's hairs
+ Tape

1. Carefully tie the two hairs together. As you tie a knot,
repeat this incantation:

> *"This lovers' knot binds me and thee,*
> *Together we will always be."*

2. Tape the hairs to the back of your headboard (or under-
neath your bed). Caution: Be sure you want your love to last.
This spell is hard to break once cast!

Passion Power Spell

rating: **nimbus**

This exciting spell increases the passion between you
and a lover—both in and out of bed. The energies raised
by this spell are very intense—are you both prepared
to enjoy the results?

Best times to perform this spell:
+ During the waxing moon
+ When either the sun or moon is in Taurus, Libra, or Scorpio
+ On Tuesdays or Fridays

Ingredients or equipment needed:
+ Chocolate sauce
+ Four votive candles (1 yellow, 1 red, 1 green, 1 blue)

1. Invite your partner to accompany you in performing this
spell to increase the love between you. Before you begin, place
the yellow candle in the east, the red one in the south, the blue
one in the west, and the green one in the north in your bedroom.

2. Light the yellow candle, then move in a clockwise direction and light the other three.

3. Undress, then use the chocolate sauce to fingerpaint
symbols that represent love on one another's bodies.

4. Lick off the chocolate. Engage in whatever sexual or sen-
sual pleasures you choose.

5. At the end of the session, extinguish the candles, beginning in the east and moving counterclockwise.

Dangerous Liaisons

rating: **nimbus**

Wishing for an encounter with a forbidden lover? This spell will help you attract the object of your affection—but there are always risks. Perform this spell with care and consider the possibilities before proceeding.

Best times to perform this spell:
+ During the waxing moon
+ When either the sun or moon is in Taurus, Libra, or Scorpio
+ On Tuesdays or Fridays

Ingredients or equipment needed:
+ A red votive candle in a candleholder
+ A lock of your beloved's hair
+ A lock of your own hair
+ A drop of your beloved's blood, on a piece of paper or cloth
+ A drop of your own blood, on a piece of paper or cloth

1. Put the candle in a place where it can safely burn for a few hours and light it.

2. Drop the hair into the candle flame and watch it burn while you say your wish aloud.

3. Drop the pieces of blood-spotted paper (or cloth) into the candle flame and watch them burn while you say your wish aloud.

4. Stare into the flame and envision your wish coming true.

5. Allow the candle to finish burning completely—don't blow it out.

Spell to Reconnect with an Old Lover

rating: **smoky**

The mind is the source of all magickal power.
This spell uses the creative energy of imagination to help
you hook up with a former love.

Best times to perform this spell:
- When Mercury is retrograde
- When the sun or moon is in Scorpio or Pisces
- On Fridays

1. Sit in a comfortable, quiet place where you won't be disturbed. Close your eyes, press your thumbs and index fingers together, and breathe slowly and deeply.

2. When you feel relaxed and centered, bring your old flame's face and form into your mind's eye—make the image as vivid as possible. If you know where this person lives, mentally see yourself traveling there. If you don't know where s/he lives, just hold your beloved's image in your mind and allow yourself to be drawn to him/her. Take your time and envision every step of the journey—the more details you include in your visualization, the better. Feel your love and passion growing stronger as you near the place where your lover waits. When you reach his/her home, see your lover open the door and embrace you.

3. Give your imagination free rein from this point on. Repeat this mental journey daily until you and your former flame reconnect physically.

Love Potion #9

rating: **smoky**

Enjoy this sense-ational potion with someone you love!

Best times to perform this spell:

✦ Nine days before the full moon

Ingredients or equipment needed:

✦ 9 ounces of your favorite unscented massage oil
✦ 2 drops of rose, jasmine, patchouli, or ylang-ylang essential oil
✦ 2 red rose petals, dried and crumbled finely
✦ 2 drops of apple cider
✦ 1/8 teaspoon honey, melted
✦ 1/8 teaspoon vanilla extract

1. Combine all ingredients in a glass bottle.

2. Stopper the bottle and shake it nine times.

3. Put the bottle in a place where the moonlight can shine on it for nine nights. (Don't worry if it's cloudy or raining, the moon's vibrations will permeate the potion anyway).

4. On the night of the full moon, anoint your partner's feet and hands with the oil, then let him/her anoint yours. Expand your range and massage each other's bodies with Love Potion #9 for as long as you like. Take your time and enjoy the experience!

Me and Thee Spell

rating: **smoky**

Want to propel a romantic relationship to the next level?
Be sure you're ready for commitment before you begin—
this spell isn't for dilettantes.

Best times to perform this spell:

+ During the waxing moon
+ When either the sun or moon is in Taurus or Libra
+ On Fridays

Ingredients or equipment needed:

+ A photo of you and your lover
+ A plain silver, gold, or copper ring
+ A small wooden box
+ One of your hairs
+ One of your beloved's hairs
+ A red ribbon

1. While you work, keep your mind focused on positive thoughts of you and your lover together. Place the photo of your beloved and yourself in the bottom of the wooden box.

2. Next, tie your hair and your beloved's hair around the ring, then set the ring on top of the photo. (If the hairs aren't long enough to tie, lay the ring on top of the photo and place both hairs inside the ring.)

3. Put the lid on the box, then tie the red ribbon around it, forming three knots.

4. Bury the box beneath an apple tree, or in a place that has a positive, special meaning for you.

Chalice and Dagger Ritual

rating: **smoky**

This ritual symbolizes the union of male and female— perform it with a partner to strengthen your love.

Best times to perform this spell:

+ During the waxing moon
+ When the sun or moon is in Taurus or Libra
+ On Tuesdays or Fridays

Ingredients or equipment needed:

+ A chalice or goblet
+ An athame or kitchen knife
+ Wine or apple cider

1. Pour some wine in a ritual chalice (if you have one) or goblet. The woman holds the chalice, whose shape symbolizes the womb—source of feminine creative energy. The man holds a ritual dagger known as an athame (if you have one) or a kitchen knife, which symbolizes the penis—source of masculine creative energy.

2. As the man inserts the athame's blade into the chalice, both people say together:

*"As the union of Goddess and God, earth and sky, yin and yang
creates the Universe and all life therein,
let our own union create
all the blessings and happiness we desire and deserve."*

3. Remove the dagger and lay it aside.

4. Focus on each other and your love while you drink the wine or cider together.

naughty

The Elixir of Love

rating: **nimbus**

This loving cup includes an ingredient known
in some magickal circles as "elixir."

Best times to perform this spell:

+ During the waxing moon
+ When the sun or moon is in Taurus, Libra, or Scorpio
+ On Tuesdays or Fridays

Ingredients or equipment needed:

+ A chalice or goblet
+ Wine or apple cider
+ Male and female sexual fluids

1. Engage in sexual intercourse.

2. Pour some wine or apple cider in a ritual chalice or goblet.

3. Add a few drops of "elixir"—the mixture of male and female sexual fluids—to the chalice.

4. Focus on each other and your love while you drink the "potentized" wine (or cider) together.

Spell to Keep a Lover from Wandering

rating: **nimbus**

This spell uses "sympathetic magick" to bind two people together. Be forewarned, however, once in place the bond is difficult to break.

Best times to perform this spell:

+ During the new moon
+ When the sun or moon is in Taurus, Scorpio, or Capricorn
+ On Saturdays

Ingredients or equipment needed:

+ Clippings of your lover's hair
+ Several of your own hairs
+ Clippings of your lover's fingernails
+ A garment your lover has worn
+ A silk scarf you've worn
+ Colored markers
+ All-purpose glue
+ A simple figurine made of wax, cloth, wood, or other material

1. Fabricate or buy a simple figurine.

2. Hold the figurine before you and say, "I name you [lover's name]."

3. Glue your lover's hair on the figurine's head and his/her fingernails on the figurine's fingers.

4. Draw "features" to make the figurine resemble your lover—eyes of the appropriate color, distinguishing birthmarks, scars, tattoos, etc.

5. Dress it in cloth from your lover's garment.

6. Tie your own hair around the figurine's ankles and say:

> *"I am yours and you are mine.*
> *Our paths shall evermore entwine.*
> *None can charm you away from me*
> *And we shall always happy be."*

7. Wrap the figurine in your scarf and conceal it in a safe spot in your bedroom.

Forget-Me-Not Spell

rating: **smoky**

Make certain a lover remembers you always—this spell will keep you in your beloved's thoughts night and day.

Best times to perform this spell:
+ During the waxing moon
+ When the sun or moon is in Taurus or Libra
+ On Fridays

Ingredients or equipment needed:
+ A sewing needle
+ One (or more) of your hairs
+ A garment your lover wears often

1. Thread your hair through the needle's eye.

2. Carefully sew your hair into your beloved's garment, and with each stitch, repeat this incantation:

> *"Forget me not, for I am near*
> *Every day of every year.*
> *My love abides within this hair*
> *Carry it with you everywhere."*

3. Stitch as many hairs into as many garments as you wish. When you've finished, return your lover's clothing to him/her.

Light My Fire

rating: **smoky**

Spark passion in the heart of someone new or fan the
flames in an existing relationship.

Best times to perform this spell:
+ During the waxing moon
+ When the sun or moon is in Leo or Libra
+ On Tuesdays or Fridays

Ingredients or equipment needed:
+ A red candle
+ A candleholder
+ A ballpoint pen
+ Love Lotion (see page 15, Nice)
+ Matches
+ A ring large enough to slide over the candle

1. With the pen, carve your name and your partner's on the
candle, so that the letters are alternated and interspersed. For
example, Bill and Sue would be written: B S I U L E L.

2. Rub some Love Lotion on the candle, then slide the ring
onto it—the symbolism is obvious.

3. Place the candle in the holder and light it. As you stare
into the flame, chant the word created by your joint names.
Envision a union between you and your partner.

4. When you can no longer concentrate on this spell, snuff
out the candle.

5. Repeat daily until the candle burns down to the ring.

6. Remove the ring and place it under your mattress to "fire
up" a romance.

Love Letters

rating: **smoky**

Like the preceding spell, this one entwines the letters
in your name with those of your beloved's to strengthen
the link between you.

Best times to perform this spell:
+ During the waxing moon
+ When the sun or moon is in Taurus or Libra
+ On Fridays

Ingredients or equipment needed:
+ A piece of pink or red paper
+ A ballpoint pen with purple ink
+ Love Lotion (see page 15, Nice)
+ A red ribbon

1. With the ballpoint pen, write your name and your partner's on the paper, so that the letters are interspersed. For
example, Bill and Sue would be written: B S I U L E L

2. Put a dot of Love Lotion on each corner of the paper,
then fold it three times. With each dot and each fold, repeat
the word that's formed when your names are merged this
way.

3. Tie the red ribbon around the folded paper, making six
knots in the ribbon.

4. Envision you and your partner being as interconnected
as the letters in the magick word formed by your joined
names. Place the paper under your pillow, mail it to your
beloved, or add it to the following Gemstone Love Talisman.

Gemstone Love Talisman

rating: **smoky**

The shapes and energies of these two gemstones represent the male and female—combine them to attract an exciting new romance or to increase the passion in an existing relationship.

Best times to perform this spell:

+ During the waxing moon
+ When the sun or moon is in Taurus or Libra
+ On Tuesdays or Fridays

Ingredients or equipment needed:

+ A donut-shaped piece of rose quartz
+ An obelisk-shaped piece of carnelian
+ A red cloth pouch
+ Rose, jasmine, or musk incense
+ Matches

1. Put both stones in the pouch where they can nestle together and work their magick. If you wish, add the Love Letters described in the previous spell.

2. Light the incense and hold your talisman in the smoke to charge it (or use the method on page 71). Envision your lover and you joined in a passionate embrace.

3. Place the pouch under your mattress to draw the love you desire into your life.

Bed of Roses

rating: **smoky**

Heighten your passion with this romantic spell.

Best times to perform this spell:

+ During the waxing moon
+ When the sun or moon is in Taurus or Libra
+ On Tuesdays or Fridays

Ingredients or equipment needed:

+ 6 red roses

1. Pluck the petals off the roses and scatter them on your sheets, while you state your wishes aloud.

2. Make love in this "bed of roses" to intensify the love in your relationship.

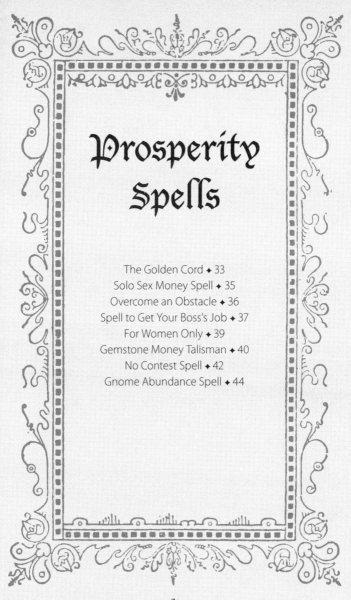

Prosperity Spells

The Golden Cord

Combine your creative energy with a partner's
to fuel this exciting spell.

Best times to perform this spell:
+ During the full moon
+ When the sun or moon is in Taurus
+ On Thursdays

Ingredients or equipment needed:
+ A gold-colored cord
+ 12 candles in rainbow colors
+ 12 candleholders
+ Matches

1. Acquire a gold-colored cord that's as long as you are from the tips of your toes to the tips of your fingers when your arm is fully extended above your head.

2. Arrange the candles in a circle around the space where you will perform this spell.

3. Enter the circle with your partner, bringing the golden cord with you.

4. Light the candles, beginning in the east and continuing in a clockwise direction until all are burning.

5. Make love, coordinating your activity so that one person reaches orgasm first.

6. At the moment of orgasm, the other person ties a few knots in the cord. Then, as the second person reaches orgasm, the partner ties a few knots.

continued

7. Throughout the entire experience, focus your minds on the objective: to attract money. Your intention and energy are tied into the knots.

8. When you're finished, snuff out all the candles beginning at the east and working counterclockwise. Whenever you need money, open one of the knots and release the energy.

Solo Sex Money Spell

rating: **nimbus**

When a suitable partner isn't available (or wanted), this spell taps your own creative energy to attract prosperity.

Best times to perform this spell:
+ During the waxing moon
+ When the sun or moon is in Taurus or Scorpio
+ On Thursdays

Ingredients or equipment needed:
+ None required, sex toys optional

1. Focus is the key to success with this spell—keep your mind clearly fixed on your objective and don't allow other fantasies to intrude.

2. Engage in self-stimulation for as long as you like. At the moment of orgasm, visualize paper money flowing toward you from all directions, until it forms a soft comforter around you and you are "rolling in money."

Overcome an Obstacle

rating: **smoky (be careful with the dagger!)**

Is something standing in the way of your financial or career success? Perhaps you'll have to remove the obstacle before you can make progress. Whether the obstacle is an attitude or something physical, this spell can help you to overcome it.

Best times to perform this spell:

+ During the waning moon
+ When the sun or moon is in Scorpio
+ On Saturdays

Ingredients or equipment needed:

+ An athame or kitchen knife

1. Hold the athame (a ritual dagger) or knife in your right hand.

2. Close your eyes and imagine you are in a jungle choked with vines and brush.

3. Hold the dagger out in front of you and make slashing motions as you symbolically cut away the thick growth that's blocking your path. Chop your way into a small clearing, where you see a suitcase full of money. Pick up the suitcase and take it with you. Warning: If the obstacle is a person, don't envision yourself slicing up him or her with your dagger—in your mind's eye picture vines, which represent the situation rather than the individual.

Spell to Get Your Boss's Job

rating: **smoky**

Could you do a better job than your boss? Let magick help you get the promotion you deserve.

Best times to perform this spell:
+ During the waxing moon
+ When the sun or moon is in Leo or Capricorn
+ On Thursdays or Sundays

Ingredients or equipment needed:
+ A camera and film
+ A picture of yourself, looking happy and confident
+ A pen
+ One (or more) of your hairs

1. Photograph your boss's office or workspace when s/he isn't there, then paste a picture of yourself on the photo. Or, have a trusted friend photograph you seated at your boss's desk.

2. On the back of the photo, write your name and new job title.

3. Focus your attention on the photo first thing every morning and last thing every night for one week minimum.

4. When the opportunity arises, hide the photo in your boss's office in a spot where s/he won't find it.

5. Tie your hair to the doorknob or sprinkle a few hair clippings in your boss's desk drawer.

continued

6. Say aloud:

"This office and job are now mine. [Boss's name] now takes another job for which s/he is better suited. We are both very happy and successful in our new positions."

7. Continue visualizing yourself performing your new job until you receive a promotion.

For Women Only

Ben-wa balls do double-duty in this exciting spell,
which uses your creative energy to increase
the power of a prosperity talisman.

Best times to perform this spell:
+ During the waxing moon
+ When the sun or moon is in Taurus or Scorpio
+ On Thursdays

Ingredients or equipment needed:
+ Two aventurine spheres of a size that's comfortable for you
+ A green or gold drawstring pouch
+ Personal lubricant (optional)

1. Sterilize the aventurine spheres or wash them with soap and water, and rinse them thoroughly.

2. Gently insert the spheres into your vagina. Leave them inside your body for at least eight minutes, longer if you wish.

3. Remove the spheres and slip them into the pouch—don't wash them.

4. Say aloud,

> *"My body births this magick spell*
> *By my own fluids nurtured well*
> *My wealth and success now manifest*
> *And bring to all concerned the best."*

5. Place the talisman in your purse, cash drawer, safe, or other location where it can generate money. If you know feng shui, put it in the Wealth Gua of your home or office.

Gemstone Money Talisman

rating: **nimbus**

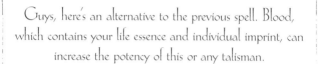

Guys, here's an alternative to the previous spell. Blood, which contains your life essence and individual imprint, can increase the potency of this or any talisman.

Best times to perform this spell:
+ During the waxing moon
+ When the sun or moon is in Taurus
+ On Thursdays

Ingredients or equipment needed:
+ A rose thorn or straight pin
+ Rubbing alcohol
+ An aventurine sphere (any size)
+ A green or gold drawstring pouch

1. Wash the aventurine sphere with soap and water.

2. Sterilize the rose thorn or pin with alcohol, then prick your finger with it.

3. Squeeze out a drop of blood and dab it on the aventurine sphere to empower it.

4. As you do this, envision your personal power activating the stone, so that it resonates with your vital energy, and chant the following incantation aloud:

> *"Blood that flows from my own heart*
> *Strengthens the magician's art.*
> *My wealth and success now manifest*
> *And bring to all concerned the best."*

5. Put a little alcohol on your finger.

6. Slip your talisman in the pouch and tie it with three knots.

7. Place the talisman in your pocket, cash drawer, safe, or other location where it can generate money. If you know feng shui, put it in the Wealth Gua of your home or office.

No Contest Spell

rating: **smoky**

Win a job, award, or contest with this colorful spell. The powerful imagery on tarot cards can help you beat out the competition.

Best times to perform this spell:
+ During the waxing moon
+ When the sun or moon is in Leo
+ On Sundays or Thursdays

Ingredients or equipment needed:
+ A deck of tarot cards
+ 9 quartz crystals

1. From a tarot deck, choose nine cards that signify qualities you need in order to triumph over all other contenders for the prize you desire.

2. Stand in the center of an area you've already cleansed with sage or incense, then lay the cards on the floor forming a circle around you.

3. Place a crystal on each card—but before you set it down, blow on the crystal and say,

> *"Bring me the qualities symbolized by this card so I can use them to advance my goals and desires."*

4. Close your eyes and imagine the energies depicted on all nine cards streaming toward you. Feel yourself soaking up the qualities that will bring you success.

5. When you're ready, open your eyes and say,

   *"I now win the [job/award/contest, etc.], in harmony
      with Divine Will and with good to all."*

6. Put the cards away. Put the crystals in a place that relates
to your wish.

Gnome Abundance Spell

rating: **smoky**

Gnomes are invisible entities who expertly handle matters such as finances and worldly goods. If you befriend them, they'll help you get all kinds of goodies—but if they don't like you they're not above playing nasty tricks.

Best times to perform this spell:
+ During the waxing moon
+ When the sun or moon is in Taurus, Virgo, or Capricorn

Ingredients or equipment needed:
+ A piece of jewelry

1. While in meditation, visualize yourself entering a cave deep in the earth. Find your way to the center, where you meet a small, troll-like creature—a gnome. Introduce yourself and be respectful. Explain that you need money or desire a particular material object, and ask the gnome to help you acquire it. Sometimes gnomes can seem grouchy or stubborn, so be patient. If you hold negative attitudes toward wealth (such as believing that money is the root of evil), the gnome probably won't come to your aid. If the gnome agrees to assist you, thank him/her and leave the cave.

2. Come out of your meditation. Take a piece of jewelry to a park or the woods and bury it near a tree or rock. Say, "Gnome, I offer this gift in thanks for your help, knowing you will bring me [whatever you seek]."

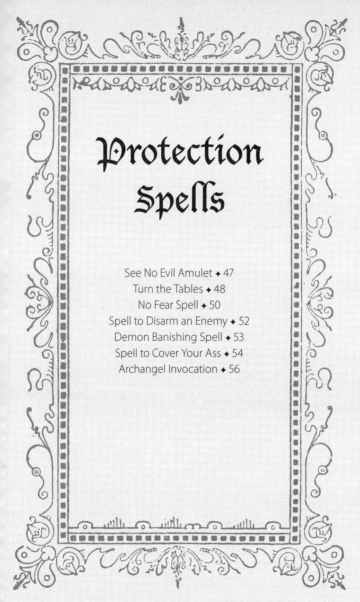

Protection Spells

See No Evil Amulet

rating: **smoky**

This spell keeps other people from seeing you when you are doing something you don't want anyone else to know about.

Best times to perform this spell:
+ During the new moon
+ When the sun or moon is in Scorpio
+ On Mondays or Saturdays

Ingredients or equipment needed:
+ A black pouch
+ A black ribbon
+ A piece of smoky quartz
+ A piece of jet, onyx, or other black gemstone
+ Heliotrope essential oil
+ Clippings of your hair and fingernails

1. Rub heliotrope oil on the stones, then slip them into the pouch.

2. Add your hair and nail clippings to the pouch.

3. Tie the black ribbon around the pouch to close it.

4. Make nine knots in the ribbon, and each time you tie a knot, repeat this incantation:

> *"Whatever I do,*
> *Wherever I go,*
> *No one will see,*
> *No one will know."*

5. Carry the pouch in your pocket or wear it around your neck whenever you want to be "invisible."

Turn the Tables

rating: **smoky**

Is someone making your life difficult? Turn the tables on that person with this clever spell.

Best times to perform this spell:

◆ Anytime

Ingredients or equipment needed:

◆ A candle
◆ A candleholder
◆ A small mirror
◆ A photo of your tormentor (if possible)
◆ Matches

1. Place the candle in its holder and set it on top of the photo at one end of a table. If you can't obtain a photo, inscribe your enemy's name on the candle—the candle represents the person who's causing you trouble.

2. Light the candle, then seat yourself at the other end of the table.

3. Hold the mirror so that it reflects the flame and say aloud:

> *"Behold, this mirror is my shield.*
> *Your wicked ways will be revealed.*
> *Any evil that you do*
> *Will instantly turn back on you."*

4. Imagine the mirror deflecting harm away from you and back onto the other person.

5. When you've finished, snuff out the candle.

6. Hang the mirror on the outside of the door to your home or office to ward off unwanted energies.

7. Melt the candle completely and bury the residue along with the photo far from your home.

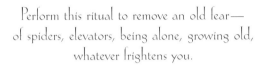

No Fear Spell

rating: **smoky**

Perform this ritual to remove an old fear—
of spiders, elevators, being alone, growing old,
whatever frightens you.

Best times to perform this spell:

+ A few days before the new moon
+ When the sun or moon is in Scorpio or Capricorn
+ On Saturdays

Ingredients or equipment needed:

+ A picture of something you fear
+ Scissors
+ A small black container
+ A trowel
+ Rescue Remedy (available in health food stores)

1. Put two drops of Rescue Remedy under your tongue about 15 minutes before you begin.

2. Gaze at the picture of something you fear. If you start to feel anxious at any time, take a few slow, deep breaths.

3. Cut the picture into tiny pieces and, as you chop it up, imagine you are destroying the fear's power over you.

4. Place the remnants in the black container, then take them to a cemetery.

5. Dig a hole and bury the container—and your fear along with it.

6. Gently press your solar plexus and repeat this affirmation three times:

"I am free of all fear. I am safe and sound at all times and in all situations."

7. Perform this spell as often as necessary until you are free of fear.

Spell to Disarm an Enemy

rating: **smoky**

Is someone trying to harm you? Block this person's power through the use of "sympathetic magick."

Best times to perform this spell:
+ During the new moon
+ When the sun or moon is in Capricorn
+ On Saturdays

Ingredients or equipment needed:
+ A simple figurine made of wax, cloth, wood, clay, or other material
+ Permanent markers
+ Duct tape
+ A shovel

1. Fabricate or purchase a simple figurine.

2. Say to the figurine, "I now name you [enemy's name]" and write the name on the figurine's chest.

3. Draw "features" to make the figurine resemble your enemy—eyes of the appropriate color, distinguishing birth-marks, scars, tattoos, etc.

4. Wrap the figurine with duct tape, until it is completely encased. As you wind the tape, repeat this incantation:

> *"I bind you tightly as can be.*
> *You have no strength to injure me."*

5. When you've finished, take the figurine to a spot far from your home and bury it deep in the ground. Note: Don't bury it at the base of a tree or near a body of water.

Demon Banishing Spell

rating: **smoky**

Whether the "demon" exists within or without, this spell drains its psychic power.

Best times to perform this spell:

+ Three nights before the new moon

Ingredients or equipment needed:

+ An empty coffee can with a plastic lid
+ 1 pound of sea salt
+ A shovel

1. Pour most of the sea salt into the coffee can and place the open can in the center of your basement.

2. Sprinkle some salt in each corner of your basement.

3. Envision the demon as a grayish cloud and see it being absorbed by the salt in the can. Say aloud:

> *"Begone now, demon, let me be.*
> *No longer can you torment me.*
> *I bind you for eternity*
> *And I shall evermore be free."*

4. On the new moon, put the lid on the coffee can and take it to a desolate place—a vacant lot, a desert, a gravel pit, the town dump—away from water, trees, people, or animals. Don't open the can! Bury it and say good riddance to the demon trapped inside.

Spell to Cover Your Ass

rating: **smoky**

Whether you've done something you shouldn't or neglected to do something you should have, this spell throws a "smoke screen" around you.

Best times to perform this spell:
+ During the new moon
+ When the sun or moon is in Scorpio

Ingredients or equipment needed:
+ Wood chips from these trees: ash, rowan, pussy willow, holly
+ Small amounts of these herbs: fennel, basil, garlic, dill, St. John's Wort, valerian, star anise
+ Seeds or petals from these flowers: peony, white snapdragon, primrose
+ An amber-colored glass bottle with stopper
+ A gray silk scarf
+ Matches

1. In a safe place (fireplace, barbecue grill) build a small fire using the wood chips, herbs, and seeds or petals.

2. When the fire has died down to ashes, hold the amber bottle above the ashes and collect some smoke. Stopper the bottle.

3. Hold the silk scarf in the smoke (don't let it catch fire!) for a few moments. Extinguish the fire.

4. The next time you need to cover your ass, open the bottle and let the smoke flow out. Imagine it swelling to form a dense cloud around you, completely hiding you from sight. Drape the scarf over your shoulders and imagine concealing yourself (and whatever you did or didn't do) with a cloak of invisibility. Note: Refill the bottle with magick smoke after each use.

Archangel Invocation

rating: **smoky**

This spell invokes the powers of the archangel Michael to help you conquer an enemy or adversary.

Best times to perform this spell:
+ When the sun or moon is in Aries
+ On Sundays

Ingredients or equipment needed:
+ A magick wand (see Appendix H)

1. Purchase a magick wand and cleanse it in water, then "charge" it using one of the methods described in this book. Or, make your own (see Lightning Strikes, page 64).

2. Go to a private spot outdoors and face south. Envision the archangel Michael standing before you wearing a red robe, holding a mighty sword.

3. Grasp your wand in both hands, arms fully extended, and point it at the vision of Michael in front of you. Feel his courage and power flowing through the wand, into your body, all the way down to your feet.

4. Say aloud:

> *"Guardian of the southern sphere*
> *I now seek your presence here.*
> *Grant me courage, speed, and might*
> *So I succeed in every fight.*
> *Your power through this wand now flows*
> *To help me vanquish all my foes."*

5. Whenever an enemy or adversary threatens you, point your wand at him/her (literally or in your imagination) and watch your foe beat a hasty retreat.

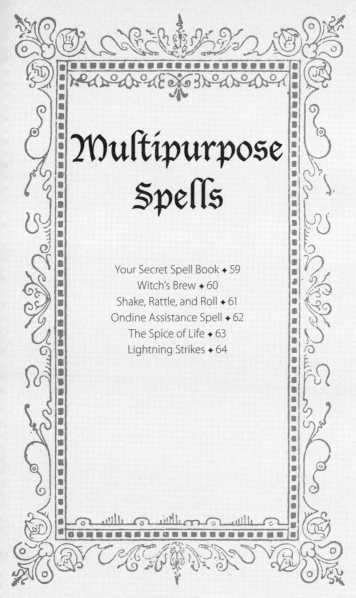

Multipurpose Spells

naughty

Your Secret Spell Book

rating: **smoky**

A grimoire or "Book of Shadows" is a magician's journal or personal "recipe book" of spells and rituals. Here's where you record all your secrets.

Best times to perform this spell:
+ After each spell or ritual

Ingredients or equipment needed:
+ A bound journal, loose-leaf binder with paper, or other notebook
+ A pen

1. Each time you perform a magick spell or ritual, write down in detail what you did, when you did it, for whom, what ingredients you used, and what happened. Include any other details you think might be relevant or informative.

2. Continue updating your Book of Shadows as your magickal knowledge grows. Important: Don't show your grimoire to anyone else and keep it in a safe place so it doesn't fall into the wrong hands!

Witch's Brew

rating: **nimbus**

How trusting—and trustworthy—are you?
Perform this advanced spell with a lover, friend,
relative, or magickal partner.

Best times to perform this spell:

◆ Depends on your intentions—see Appendix D

Ingredients or equipment needed:

◆ Depends on your intentions—see Appendices

1. Once you've mastered the art of mixing magick potions, you can begin concocting your own original "witch's brews" for special purposes. With a partner you trust, agree that each of you will formulate a potion for the other. Ideally, the potions should be designed to help the other person overcome a problem or attract a benefit, but it's entirely up to you! Don't tell one another what's in your potions or what results these mysterious brews are likely to produce.

2. Create your potions separately, in private, then exchange them and drink them together. Then wait and see what happens…

Shake, Rattle, and Roll

rating: **smoky**

Has your life lost its spark? Do you feel stuck in the doldrums, trapped by responsibilities, lethargy, or fear? This spell lets you shake things up—but be prepared for some surprises.

Best times to perform this spell:

◆ When the sun or moon is in Aquarius

Ingredients or equipment needed:

◆ A rattle

1. Go to the place where you wish to effect a change (or to a room in your home that symbolizes the area of your life that you intend to change). If you'd like to change your job, for example, do this spell in your workplace; if you want to shake up your love life, do it in your bedroom.

2. Take a few moments to open your heart and mind.

3. Start in the east and begin shaking the rattle. Slowly move in a clockwise direction around the area, continually shaking the rattle down near the floor, up over your head, anyway you choose. Sing, chant, shout, or dance about if you like.

4. When you've made a complete circle and are confident you've broken up all the old energies in the space, move to the center. Shake the rattle around yourself to break up old patterns and stimulate your auric field. End with the words, "This spell is done for the good of all."

Ondine Assistance Spell

rating: **smoky**

Ondines are invisible beings who are experts in the field of relationships and other emotional issues. If you befriend them, they'll help you handle problems in these areas—but if they don't like you, they can be tricksters!

Best times to perform this spell:

✦   When either the sun or moon is in Cancer, Scorpio, or Pisces
✦   On Mondays

Ingredients or equipment needed:

✦   Perfume or essential oil

1. Go to a beautiful body of water—a stream, lake, waterfall, the ocean—and sit quietly beside it. Invite the ondines to meet with you.

2. Pour perfume or essential oil into the water. Say,

"Ondines, I offer you this gift and request your help with [whatever you seek]."

3. You may see them as bubbles, eddies, or nebulous shapes in the water, or you might only sense their presence. Introduce yourself and be respectful. Explain the situation(s) you are concerned about and ask for their assistance. For the most part, they are compassionate beings, but if you hold negative attitudes toward your emotions, the ondines probably won't have anything to do with you. Note: After they've helped you with your problem(s), show gratitude by giving them more perfume to enlist their continued friendship.

The Spice of Life

rating: **smoky**

Add spice to your life with this delicious spell.
It gets a "smoky" rating because you might get too much of
a good thing—remember the old saying, be careful what
you wish for. . .

Best times to perform this spell:

+ When the sun or moon is in Aries or Aquarius
+ On Tuesdays

Ingredients or equipment needed:

+ A spice cake
+ One whole clove

1. Play "hot" music, such as salsa, while you make a spice
cake using your favorite recipe or a packaged mix.

2. Stir one whole clove into the batter. Ice the finished cake
with red icing, while you repeat this incantation:

> "Magick cake, so sweet and spicy
> Make my life both rich and dicey.
> Change my nights from dull and mild
> Make them joyful, fun, and wild.
> Add excitement to my days
> In myriad delightful ways,
> With good to all, now and always."

3. If you wish, decorate it with candy red hots, pictures or
words that represent your intentions, or other fiery, spicy
symbols. Eat the entire cake yourself—not all in one sitting, though! As you eat it, keep your mind focused on your
desires. When you bite into the clove, your spell will activate
and your intentions will begin to manifest.

Lightning Strikes

rating: **smoky**

A magick wand becomes a lightning rod in this spell, enabling you to direct tremendous power toward all your objectives.

Best times to perform this spell:

+ Just before a thunderstorm

Ingredients or equipment needed:

+ A slender oak branch
+ A piece of copper wire
+ A brass tack
+ A hammer

1. Cut a branch 6 to 12 inches long from an oak tree (ask the tree's permission first).

2. Remove the bark. Hammer the tack into the end where you will hold the wand.

3. Before a thunderstorm begins, fasten the wand with the copper wire to something that could feasibly be struck by lightning—a tree, metal pole, etc.

4. After the storm is over, remove the wand. If you wish, you can decorate it with symbols that represent power. Or, charge it with blood or "elixir" (see pages 23 and 71).

5. Whenever you want to strengthen your willpower or direct energy toward an intention, hold the wand in both hands with your right thumb on the brass tack and aim the wand at the sky. Imagine lighting flowing down into the wand. Then point the wand wherever you wish to send energy while you visualize the lightning's power streaming out the end of the wand.

naughty

Miscellaneous Spells

Magick Sigil

rating: **depends on your intention**

A sigil is a symbol or sign that contains within it a magickal intention. One type of sigil combines letters to create a picture of something you desire. Only you can understand your secret code—it's totally private!

Best times to perform this spell:

✦ Depends on your intention—see Appendix D

Ingredients or equipment needed:

✦ Paper in a color that relates to your intention—see Appendix A
✦ A pen or pencil

1. Think of a word that represents your objective, for instance prosperity or creativity.

2. On a piece of colored paper, arrange the letters into a design that you find appealing. You can write them in script or print them, uppercase or lowercase. It doesn't matter if the letters are right-side up, upside down, forward, backward—be creative. If the word contains the same letter twice, such as P in prosperity, you only need to write it once.

3. Keep your mind focused on your intention while you work. If you wish, you can empower your intention by using the sigil in the following spell.

4. Display the finished sigil in a place where you'll see it often—your subconscious will recognize its meaning. Sigils can also be included in talismans and amulets.

Sigil Sex Spell

rating: **nimbus**

This spell uses the power of sexual pleasure to activate the secret wishes you've encoded into a sigil. You can perform this spell solo or with a partner.

Best times to perform this spell:

✦ Depends on your intentions—see Appendix D

Ingredients or equipment needed:

✦ A sigil

1. Draw a sigil according to the Magick Sigil spell on page 67.

2. Place the sigil where you can see it easily—hang it on a wall or the ceiling, for instance.

3. Engage in sexual activity. At the moment of orgasm, stare at the sigil. You don't have to think about what it means, your subconscious knows even if your conscious mind is temporarily "on hold." The energy you've raised will fuel the intentions embodied in the sigil. Leave the sigil in place or put it away until another time—your choice.

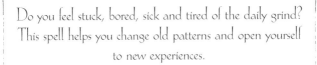

Unblocking Spell to Change Your Life
rating: **smoky**

Do you feel stuck, bored, sick and tired of the daily grind? This spell helps you change old patterns and open yourself to new experiences.

Best times to perform this spell:
+ During the new moon
+ When the sun or moon is in Scorpio or Aquarius
+ On Tuesdays

Ingredients or equipment needed:
+ 5 items that symbolize things you want to be free of

1. Go through your closets, drawers, file cabinets, attic, basement, etc. and select five things that represent old ideas, habits, emotions, or behaviors you wish to eliminate—anything from a pack of cigarettes to your wedding gown from your first marriage.

2. Get rid of these objects, right now! Give them to charity, burn them, bury them, or flush them down the toilet—the more dramatic, the better.

3. As you dump these items, visualize yourself releasing the attitudes, attachments, and feelings they symbolize.

4. Repeat this spell each month, until you notice a change in your situation. Nature abhors a vacuum, so don't just leave a big hole in your life—make sure you fill the gap with something positive. Warning: You may experience some discomfort or uncertainty as you shed the old "stuff"—give yourself time to adjust.

Beltane Fertility Ritual

rating: **smoky**

Beltane (May 1) is an ancient pagan holiday that celebrates fertility of all kinds. This Beltane ritual encourages creativity in every form, from painting to pregnancy.

Best times to perform this spell:
+ May 1

Ingredients or equipment needed:
+ Motherwort leaves (dried)
+ 9 acorns
+ 9 caraway seeds
+ 9 fennel seeds
+ A coral necklace
+ 9 seashells
+ Oak logs and kindling
+ Cedar chips
+ Matches

1. Using oak logs, kindling, and cedar chips, build two fires far enough apart that you can walk safely between them.

2. Drop the motherwort, acorns, caraway, and fennel into the flames.

3. Wear the coral necklace and fill your pockets with seashells.

4. Walk slowly back and forth between the fires while you envision yourself creating whatever it is you wish to bring forth into the world. (Traditionally, lovemaking and revelry are part of the Beltane festivities—children conceived on this holiday are said to belong to the Goddess.)

Charge a Charm

rating: **nimbus**

Sexual fluids can be used to "charge" a talisman or amulet with extra power. Sometimes called "elixir" in magickal circles, the mixture of male and female body fluids contains a powerful creative energy that can increase the potency of any charm, especially one designed for love or prosperity.

Best times to perform this spell:

+ Depends on your intention—see Appendix D

Ingredients or equipment needed:

+ A talisman or amulet you wish to charge
+ Sexual fluids

1. Engage in sexual intercourse with your partner. Make sure you are both in agreement about the magickal intention you wish to "birth."

2. When you've finished, collect a small amount of your mixed fluids and smear a little on an amulet or talisman (such as The Golden Cord on page 33 or Gemstone Love Talisman on page 29). As you do this, envision your personal power activating the charm, so that it resonates with your creative energy, and chant the following incantation aloud:

> *"We've joined our bodies in this rite*
> *To give this magick charm great might.*
> *Charged by passion's glorious fire*
> *It brings us now our hearts' desire."*

3. Store the magick charm in a safe place or display it where you'll see it often, until your dreams materialize.

Glamour Spell to Hide Your Age

rating: **smoky**

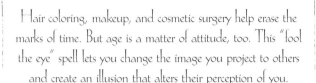

Hair coloring, makeup, and cosmetic surgery help erase the marks of time. But age is a matter of attitude, too. This "fool the eye" spell lets you change the image you project to others and create an illusion that alters their perception of you.

Best times to perform this spell:

✦ During the new moon

Ingredients or equipment needed:

✦ A hula hoop

1. Lay the hula hoop on the floor and step inside the circle.

2. Close your eyes and envision a beam of pink light extending from the heavens down to your feet, completely encasing you.

3. Grab some of the light in your hands, then rub your palms together. Gently rub your light-enriched palms upward over your neck and face. Imagine you are wiping away wrinkles and infusing your skin with youthful vitality. Do this three times.

4. Next, reach down and grasp the hula hoop with both hands. Slowly raise it until you are holding it above your head with your arms fully extended. Then slowly lower the hoop to the floor while you visualize the signs of age falling away and your body being suffused with rejuvenating light. Do this three times.

5. When you've finished, step outside the hoop. Envision the pink light still surrounding you wherever you go. Repeat monthly.

Preferential Treatment Spell

rating: **smoky**

Whether you hope to win a legal decision, land a job, or get a good grade on a paper, this spell wins you preferential treatment.

Best times to perform this spell:
- During the waxing moon
- On Thursdays

Ingredients or equipment needed:
- An orange candle and candleholder
- 2 straight pins
- Sandalwood or cedar essential oil
- A ballpoint pen
- Matches

1. With the pen, inscribe "success" in the upper third of the candle then rub oil on the candle.

2. Stick the pins into the candle, one-third of the way down from the tip.

3. Light the candle and gaze into the flame, while you concentrate on achieving a successful outcome.

4. When the candle has burned down to the pins, extinguish it and remove the pins.

5. Put one pin in a piece of clothing you'll wear when you go for a job interview, appear in court, take a test, etc.

continued

6. Put the other pin in something that belongs to the person who'll decide your "fate"—his/her clothing, briefcase, car. If that's not possible, stick the pin in a sheet of paper the other person will handle, in the chair where s/he will sit, or something else s/he will come into contact with—if necessary send him/her an anonymous letter with the pin inside. Important: Be surreptitious!

Tattoo Spell

rating: **nimbus**

This spell is permanent, so be sure it's what you really want before you do it!

Best times to perform this spell:

✦ Depends on your intention—see Appendix D

Ingredients or equipment needed:

✦ A design/symbol that represents your intention
✦ A professional tattoo artist

1. Design or choose an image or symbol that graphically represents your intention. (For example, you may select the Chinese character for prosperity to bring you financial success.)

2. Have a professional tattoo artist render it on your body to keep you ever mindful of your objective.

Past Perfect
rating: **smoky**

Most people believe you can't do anything about the past, but the ordinary limits of time and space don't apply to magick. Is there something in your past you'd like to change? Here's how.

Best times to perform this spell:
+ During the new moon
+ When the sun or moon is in Scorpio

Ingredients or equipment needed:
+ Incense
+ Matches

1. Light the incense. Sit quietly, calm and center yourself, and start breathing slowly, deeply. Bring to mind a scenario from your past and watch it begin to unfold on your mental movie screen. When you get to the part you'd like to "edit," stop the action.

2. Replace what you remember happening with what you wish had happened, as if you were splicing in a new segment of film.

3. Now roll the "movie" forward, but this time see things turn out according to your alterations. Envision yourself saying and doing things differently, other people behaving differently. The more vivid and detailed you can make this visualization, the more power it will have.

4. After emerging from your meditation, continue to think and act in keeping with the revised scenario. Caution: Remember, when you change one part of the past, everything connected with it changes, too.

Scrying Spell to See the Future

rating: **smoky**

It may take some practice to learn to relax and allow visions to come to you. Trust your intuition and pay attention to what you feel as well as what you see.

Best times to perform this spell:

+ During the new moon
+ When the sun or moon is in Cancer, Scorpio, or Pisces
+ On Mondays

Ingredients or equipment needed:

+ A cauldron or large dark bowl filled with water
+ A broom straw
+ 2 cloves, crushed
+ A rose thorn or common pin
+ Rubbing alcohol

1. Fill the cauldron or bowl with water and sprinkle the crushed cloves in it.

2. Sterilize the thorn or pin and your finger with rubbing alcohol, then prick your finger and squeeze a drop of blood into the water.

3. Make three, slow, gentle clockwise circles in the water with the broom straw. Gaze into the water without skepticism or preconceptions. Allow impressions about your future to arise into your awareness—don't censor or analyze, just keep an open mind and an open heart. Gaze as long as you like.

4. When you're finished, empty the water, and write down what you experienced.

Smoke and Mirrors

rating: **smoky**

Who were you in a past lifetime? This spell awakens your inner sight and helps you travel back in time.

Best times to perform this spell:

+ During the new moon
+ When the sun or moon is in Scorpio or Pisces
+ On Mondays

Ingredients or equipment needed:

+ A black candle
+ A candleholder
+ A mirror
+ Citrus, eucalyptus, or cinnamon incense
+ An incense holder
+ Matches

1. Set the candle and incense (in their holders) on a surface in front of a mirror and light them. Turn off other forms of illumination.

2. As the candlelight flickers and the smoke swirls in front of the mirror, gaze at your reflection. Say aloud:

> *"Shadow and light*
> *expand my sight.*
> *Open a door*
> *To a time before*
> *And let me see*
> *A different me."*

3. Continue looking at your reflection for as long as you like, while your mind drifts back in time. Notice changes in your expression, features, coloring, etc. Pay attention to impressions, emotions, or thoughts that arise, too. Don't censor yourself—sometimes strange ideas can be clues to a past personality.

4. When you've finished, extinguish the candle and write down your experiences.

Blood, Sweat, and Tears Spell

rating: **nimbus**

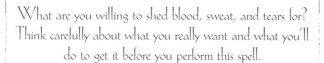

What are you willing to shed blood, sweat, and tears for? Think carefully about what you really want and what you'll do to get it before you perform this spell.

Best times to perform this spell:

✦ Depends on your intentions—see Appendix D

Ingredients or equipment needed:

✦ A chalice or glass
✦ Spring water, apple cider, or wine
✦ A drop of blood
✦ A drop of sweat
✦ A tear

1. Fill a ritual chalice (or goblet) with water, cider, or wine.

2. Prick your finger and squeeze a single drop of blood into the chalice. Add a drop of sweat and one tear.

3. Stir the mixture with your finger three times in a clockwise direction while you focus on what you desire.

4. Be willing to do whatever is necessary to accomplish your objective. See yourself already attaining your wish. Say aloud:

> *"Blood, sweat, and tears I've spilled.*
> *My greatest wish is now fulfilled.*
> *As it's sought, so it's willed."*

5. Dot each of your seven major chakra points with the liquid, then drink the rest.

Spell to force Another's hand

rating: **smoky**

Tired of waiting for someone to act or make a decision? This spell encourages another person to show his/her hand and helps bring a matter to a conclusion.

Best times to perform this spell:
+ Three days before the full moon
+ When the sun or moon is in Aries
+ On Tuesdays

Ingredients or equipment needed:
+ A bloodstone or carnelian
+ Gold paint
+ A small paintbrush
+ Essential oil of carnation, ginger, rosemary, or sesame
+ A piece of the person's clothing

1. Wash the stone, then paint the rune "Tir" or "Teiwaz" (which looks like an arrow) on it.

2. Place the stone in the sun until the paint dries.

3. Rub essential oil on the stone and wrap it in a scrap of the person's clothing. If you are friendly with the other person, give him/her the talisman before the moon is full and instruct him/her to keep it nearby at all times. If you aren't on good terms (let's say you're trying to get your estranged husband to sign divorce papers), put the stone in his/her home, car, workplace, or yard. Or, if you know feng shui, place it in the part of your own home that corresponds to that individual. Caution: This spell motivates the person, but there's no guarantee s/he'll ultimately do what you want.

Writing into Being

rating: **smoky**

You really can script your own life—the secret is to clearly and vividly imagine what you want to happen, then fuel your vision with emotion, willpower, and determination.

Best times to perform this spell:

◆ Anytime (may take several days or weeks)

Ingredients or equipment needed:

◆ Paper and pen, computer, or typewriter

1. Use your creative power to write a story about yourself, in which everything you desire happens just the way you want it to. Be very specific and tell your story with as much detail, feeling, and richness as possible. Get involved in what you're doing—really "live" the adventure you are imagining. Take your time and enjoy the process. Keep an open mind and allow yourself to be guided by inspiration as you work. Don't critique yourself or worry about the artistic merit of what you're writing—you don't have to show it to anyone else. The important thing is to realize you are designing your own destiny, and do it with passion, joy, clarity, and confidence. Put your finished story in a decorative binder, perhaps one that you've embellished with magickal symbols and imagery. Read it often to make your wishes manifest more quickly.

Appendix A
What Colors Should You Use in Magick Spells?

Colors play a part in many magick spells. Keep these color correspondences in mind when you are using candles, ribbons or cords, "mojo" bags, clothing, or images in your spells.

Use This Color	If Your Spell Involves
red	passion, vitality, courage
orange	energy, action, enthusiasm, confidence, expansion
yellow	creativity, optimism, happiness
green	healing, growth, fertility, prosperity
light blue	purity, serenity, mental clarity, relief from pain
royal blue	loyalty, insight, inspiration, independence
indigo	intuition, mental focus, inducing visions
purple	wisdom, spirituality, power
white	purity, clearing, wholeness, protection
black	power, banishing, setting boundaries
pink	love, friendship, affection, joy, self-love
brown	grounding, permanence, stability

Appendix B
Magickal Plants

Because they are living entities, plants possess magickal powers that can help you in spellworking. For centuries, wise men and women have prepared botanical charms, lotions, potions, and remedies for every imaginable purpose. Here are just a few you may want to try. (*Note*: Some of these plants are poisonous, can irritate the skin, or produce allergic reactions, so use with care.)

If This Is Your Intention	Use These Plants
love	rose, jasmine, red clover, myrtle, orchid, ylang-ylang, peach, apple, raspberry, strawberry, passion flower
prosperity	pine, cedar, mint, sunflower, sandalwood, marigold, parsley, moneyplant, saffron, asparagus
protection	basil, fennel, sage, ash, peony, snapdragon, verbena, pussy willow, fern, star anise, rowan, garlic
intuition/ insight	narcissus, lavender, wisteria, ginger, lily of the valley, lotus
purification	sage, pine, rosemary, aloe
peace of mind	lemon balm, lavender, iris, chamomile
courage/ strength	pepper, gentian, loosestrife, beech, pine, oak, mustard, chives, ivy

What Gemstones Should You Use in Magick Spells?

Long before they were prized for their monetary value, gemstones were used in magickal amulets and talismans.

If This Is Your Intention	Use These Stones
love/friendship	rose quartz, coral, opal, diamond, emerald, pearl, peridot
prosperity	aventurine, jade, tiger's eye, turquoise, star sapphire
protection	amber, jade, malachite, tourmaline
healing	jade, jasper, agate, bloodstone, amber, pearl
intuition/insight	amethyst, lapis lazuli, moonstone, opal, aquamarine, sapphire, pearl
stability/grounding	onyx, hematite, jet, obsidian, smoky quartz
courage/vitality	carnelian, ruby, topaz, garnet, diamond, bloodstone
career success/fame	ruby, topaz, garnet, diamond, sapphire, aventurine
to enhance any spell	clear quartz crystal

Appendix D
When Should You Do Magick Spells?

Day	Planetary Ruler	Do Magick Spells For
Sunday	Sun	creativity, leadership, fame
Monday	Moon	home, family, intuition, fertility
Tuesday	Mars	sports, vitality, action, sex, men
Wednesday	Mercury	communication, intellect, travel
Thursday	Jupiter	growth, luck, travel, prosperity
Friday	Venus	love, joint ventures, women
Saturday	Saturn	limits, reduction, permanence

Moon Phase	Do Magick Spells For
New moon	beginnings
Waxing moon	growth, attraction, increase
Full moon	recognition, rewards, completion, clarity, fulfillment
Waning moon	reduction, endings

When the Sun or Moon Is In	Do Magick Spells That Involve
Aries	courage, sex, men, sports, vitality, action, beginnings
Taurus	prosperity, fertility, creativity, love, sex, property, gardening
Gemini	short trips, mental pursuits, education, neighbors, siblings
Cancer	home, protection, family, children, women
Leo	career success, fame, creativity, leadership, games of chance
Virgo	health, job-related matters, coworkers, pets
Libra	love, creativity, legal issues, social standing, peace
Scorpio	power, sex, insight/intuition, investments, other people's money, transformation, over-coming obstacles
Sagittarius	long-distance travel, growth, spiritual matters, education
Capricorn	business, stability, protection, financial security, endings, boundaries, banishing
Aquarius	friends, groups, change, insight
Pisces	creativity, intuition, dreams or visions, ocean voyages, endings

Appendix E
What Numbers Should You Use in Magick Spells?

In our everyday world, numbers help us count and quantify, but in the world of magick, numbers have deeper, symbolic meanings. In some occult traditions, numbers were used in esoteric texts to convey secret knowledge. Many spells draw on the hidden significance of numbers—keep the following meanings in mind when you are tying knots, lighting candles, deciding how many ingredients to put into a talisman, etc.

Number	Secret Meaning
1	beginnings, individuality, focused energy
2	partnerships, joint ventures, union of opposites, balance
3	change, creativity, action/activation
4	stability, form, material goods
5	dispersion, instability, movement, communication
6	give and take, cooperation, fertility
7	inner peace, wholeness, development, contemplation
8	manifestation, wealth, work, permanence
9	growth, fulfillment, fortune, transitions, endings
0	unity, wholeness, completion, protection

Appendix F
What Cards Should You Use in Magick Spells?

The vivid images on tarot cards can be used in magick spells to focus your mind and produce results. If you don't own a tarot deck, you can substitute cards from a regular playing deck.

If This Is Your Intention	Use These Cards
love	The Lovers, Ace of Cups, Ace of Wands, 2 of Cups, 6 of Cups, 10 of Cups, Ace of Hearts, 10 of Hearts, Queen of Hearts
prosperity	Emperor, Ace of Pentacles, 9 of Pentacles, 10 of Pentacles, Queen of Pentacles, King of Pentacles, Ace of Diamonds, 9 of Diamonds, 10 of Diamonds, Queen of Diamonds, King of Diamonds
protection/ security	Strength, 9 of Wands, 9 of Clubs
good luck	Wheel of Fortune, The Star, 9 of Cups, 9 of Hearts
intuition/ insight	High Priestess, The Moon, The Sun, The Magician, Queen of Hearts
health/vitality	Strength, The Sun, King of Clubs
career success/fame	Emperor, Empress, The Sun, King of Wands, Queen of Wands, King of Clubs, Queen of Clubs

If This Is Your Intention	Use These Cards
victory/achievement	The Chariot, The World, 6 of Wands, 6 of Clubs
travel/adventure	The Fool, Knight of Wands, Joker, Jack of Clubs
domestic happiness	4 of Wands, 4 of Clubs
legal matters	Justice, Hierophant
peace of mind	Temperance, The World, The Hermit, Strength
power	The Magician, The Emperor, The Empress
intellect/communication	King of Swords, Queen of Swords, Ace of Swords, King of Spades, Queen of Spades, Ace of Spades
creativity	High Priestess, Empress, Queen of Wands, Ace of Wands, Queen of Hearts, Ace of Hearts

Astrology and Magick

Astrology plays a role in many magick spells and rituals. Birthstones, for instance, are gems that resonate with the vibrations of the zodiac signs. Performing spells during certain moon phases can enhance their power. The lists below show the areas of life that correspond to the twelve signs of the zodiac and the twelve houses of a birth chart.

Zodiac Sign	Correspondences
Aries	men, sports, conflict, vitality, action, beginnings
Taurus	money, gardening, art, music, fertility, sensuality
Gemini	communication, short trips, mental pursuits
Cancer	home, family, children, women, real estate
Leo	self-expression, leadership, leisure, games of chance, love affairs
Virgo	health, work, coworkers, pets
Libra	partnerships, legal issues, art, socializing, beauty
Scorpio	hidden matters, investments, other people's money, transformation, sex, the occult
Sagittarius	long-distance travel, higher education, religion
Capricorn	business, authority figures, structure, elders, boundaries
Aquarius	friends, groups, technology, change, the future
Pisces	intuition, liquids, sleep, imagination, music, poetry

Horoscope House	Area of Life
First	self, identity, physical appearance, the body
Second	personal resources, money, physical abilities
Third	siblings, neighbors, early education, short trips
Fourth	home, family, childhood, security, core issues
Fifth	creativity, love affairs, pleasure
Sixth	work, coworkers, service, health matters
Seventh	partners (love or business), agents, advisors
Eighth	partner's money/resources, hidden abilities
Ninth	spirituality, higher knowledge, long trips, the law
Tenth	career, public image
Eleventh	friends, group activities, ideologies
Twelfth	hidden fears, innate talents, secrets, intuition

Essential and Massage Oils

Aromaland
800-933-5267
www.aromaland.com

Aura Cacia
800-437-3301
www.auracacia.com

Good Clean Fun
541-344-4483
www.sacredmomentsproducts.com

Sun's Eye
800-786-7393
www.sunseye.com

Skye Botanicals
800-666-2225
www.skyebotanicals.com

V'Tae
800-643-3001
www.vtae.com

Flower Remedies

Flower Essence Society

P.O. Box 1769
Nevada City, CA 95959
www.flowersociety.org

Nelson Bach, USA

Wilmington, MA 01887

Sage and Smudging Products

Spirit Dancer Sage

800-SAGE-007

Light Stones

800-82-PEACE

Gemstones and Crystals

Heaven and Earth

800-942-9423

Craftstones

760-789-1620
www.craftstones.com

Energy Stones

866-312-0829
www.energystones.com

Wegner Crystal Mines

800-367-9888
www.wegnercrystalmines.com

Tarot Cards

U.S. Games Systems
800-544-2637
www.usgamesinc.com

Llewellyn Publications
800-THE-MOON
www.llewellyn.com

Specialty Candles

Lunar Cycle Candles
530-546-5470

Coventry Candles
800-810-3837

Sweet Spirit Candles
888-871-9001
www.sweetspiritcandles.com

Shadow and Light
800-997-4236
www.shadowandlightinc.com

Bennington Candles
888-314-3003

Aromaland
800-933-5267
www.aromaland.com

Incense

Shoyeido
800-786-5476
www.shoyeido.com

Ravenwood
800-777-5021
www.ravenwoodspa.com

DharmaCrafts
800-794-9862
www.dharmacrafts.com

Aromaland
800-933-5267
www.aromaland.com

Magick Wands

Crystal Visions Wands
800-339-5106
www.highvibes.org

Willowroot
800-554-0113
www.realmagicwands.com

Water/Wind/Stone
505-424-9020
www.waterwindstone.com

Seeds of Light
800-378-4327
www.dreamseeds.com

Magical Delights
888-317-0887
www.magicaldelights.com

JC Enterprises
800-814-6330

Pendulums

Silver Streak
800-526-9990
www.silverstreakind.com

Crystal Courier Imports
800-397-1863
www.crystalcourier.com

Life Designs
888-773-8003

Cauldrons

Sumitra
800-728-4468
www.sumitragifts.com

Drums

Rhythm Fusion
831-426-7975
www.rhythmfusion.com

Mamadou
www.mamadou.com